Glory, glory Man United. The mighty Reds celebrate their title triumph

Glory, Glory

Manchester United ended a painful, 26-year wait to win the Championship when Alex Ferguson's class of '93 clinched the first Premier League title in May.

Comparisons with the legendary Busby side of 1967 were inevitable as the guile of Giggs...the class of Cantona...and the inspiration of Ince allowed those players to be mentioned in the same breath as Best, Law and Charlton.

Yet, while the team of today has gone some way towards emulating those heroes of yesteryear, the current crop of stars know they must add one more title to their collection

Steve Bruce and Gary Pallister form a solid - and most importantly English - central defensive partnership and they both have the experience to cope with the unique pressure of playing in Europe.

Paul Ince has matured into the best midfield player in the country and then, of course, there is Ryan Giggs.

The gifted Welshman is the most exciting player in England and his unpredictable skills will terrorise even the most resolute defence.

And one man who believes that United can lift the European Cup is Bruce, who did so much to help United win the League.

He says: "Everyone is excited at the prospect of playing in the Champions' Cup. We feel we're good enough to beat the best in Europe."

And, if they do that, Fergie's Class of '94 can justifiably take their place alongside Busby's Class of '68 in the Old Trafford Hall of Fame.

...but the best is yet to come

before they can truly be called great - the European Cup.

Busby's boys followed up their 1967 title triumph by claiming the Champions' Cup 12 months later and that's the task facing Bryan Robson & Co now.

And while the entire country appears to have been engulfed with talk of United sweeping all before them in Europe, the United skipper sounds a word of warning.

Robson says: "It's no coincidence that we finally won the League in a season when we went out of all three Cup competitions early.

"So it's going to be very difficult to have a good run in the European Cup and still challenge for the Championship."

But there's no doubt United have the pedigree to take on - and beat - the best that Europe has to offer, as they proved by winning the Cup-Winners' Cup in 1991.

In Peter Schmeichel they have the world's best 'keeper and his presence will be a huge advantage to The Reds.

Man United...

How They Compare

It's impossible to judge whether Alex Ferguson's current side really are as good as Matt Busby's great team. But we asked SHOOT's United expert Rod Tradloff what he thought, and, for him, it's Fergie's boys...just.

Alex Stepney: Soild if unspectacular, Stepney rarely made a mistake. His greatest strength was his positioning, although he was capable of extreme agility when it was required. 8

Shay Brennan: A steady, rather than brilliant full-back, Brennan's main strengths were speed of recovery, good positioning and unflappability. Also deceptively skilful on the ball. 8

Tony Dunne: Probably the best United full-back in the last 30 years. Supremely quick and strong in the tackle, Dunne always did the simple things, but did them well. 9

David Sadler: A model professional, Sadler was converted from centre-forward to centre-half but could also fill in in midfield when called upon. A good passer of the ball with a fine touch. 8

Bill Foulkes: A tower of strength in the centre of defence, Foulkes was an old-fashioned stopper who could have been carved out of granite. He was a man who could be relied on. 8

Pat Crerand: United's pass master, Crerand could land a ball on a sixpence from 60 yards. Best, Law and Charlton got all the headlines but they couldn't have done it without him. 9

Nobby Stiles: One of the most tenacious characters the game has ever seen, Nobby didn't know the meaning of defeat. He did all the work, while Crerand did all the passing. A great pairing. 9

John Aston: Struggled to live up his father's reputation, Aston was often the scapegoat with the crowd when things went wrong. But, on his day, his pace made him lethal. 7

Bobby Charlton: One of the greatest players ever to play for United, Charlton is, and always be, an Old Trafford legend. His passing and shooting were second to none. 10

Brian Kidd: Didn't achieve all he should have. He was a natural ball player with superb control, an eye for goal and a thumping shot. 8

George Best: The greatest player ever to play football in this country, it's unlikely that anyone will ever be as good. Pace, skill, bravery and goals - Bestie had it all. 10

TOTAL: 94

Peter Schmeichel: Most judges reckon he's the world's best goalkeeper and it's hard to argue. A great shot stopper and great distributor of the ball. Slight weakness on crosses. 9

Paul Parker: A pocket dynamo, Parker is virtually impossible to beat for speed. And, for a small man, he's exceptionally good in the air. Distribution lets him down. 8

Dennis Irwin: Mr Reliable, he's dead cool even under extreme pressure. A good attacking full-back who chips in with a few goals and is lethal from free-kicks. 8

Steve Bruce: Solid as a rock, he's probably the best uncapped defender in England. He'd run through brick walls for United and can be depended upon in a crisis. 9

Gary Pallister: Silky defender in the Alan Hansen mould, he's got good feet and is strong in the air. His one weakness is the occasional lapse in concentration. 8

Brian McClair: United's unsung hero, he gets through so much work up and down the field. Scores goals and makes them. The other players know just how valuable he is. 8

Paul Ince: The best player in the country last season, Ince has matured into the natural successor to Bryan Robson for both club and country. And he'll get better too. 9

Lee Sharpe: Now back to his best following injury and illness, his return to fitness was vital to United's Championship charge. Quick and strong, he's a handful for any defender. 8

Eric Cantona: Provided the missing link last season and his skills and tricks delighted the Old Trafford faithful. One of Alex Ferguson's shrewdest signings. 9

Mark Hughes: Every manager in the country would love to have Hughes in his team. He's strong, quick and his scoring record speaks for itself. One of United's main men. 9

Ryan Giggs: What can you say about Giggs? Already he's a superstar and it's frightening to think what he could achieve. He's a delight to watch and the crowd love him. 10

TOTAL: 95

RED HOT

INCE PERFECT

Paul Ince has shut his mouth and let his football do the talking.

The former East End wild child has matured into one of the best midfielders in the game and did as much as anyone to help United win the title last season.

And that new found maturity has led to Ince establishing himself in the England squad and he now looks a natural successor to Bryan Robson for both club and country.

And the former West Ham star is quick to point out the role played by Robbo in his own development.

Ince says: "Bryan has been brilliant for me. He's always talking to me and telling me what to do. His advice changed me from a cocky, streetwise kid into the player I am today."

The way he's going, Paul won't need Robson's help much longer. He's now looking every Ince a star.

PAUL INCE

REDS

GIGGS: SIMPLY THE BEST

Ryan Giggs is, quite simply, the most exciting talent to emerge in this country since George Best.

Not even Gazza made such a dramatic and immediate impact as the shy, quietly-spoken young Welshman who is surely set to rule the world.

Giggs is, naturally, being compared to former Old Trafford legend Best, but even the gifted Irishman admits: "At this rate, they'll be comparing ME to HIM."

High praise indeed but Giggs has shown that his incredible talents are worthy of such plaudits. Already, AC Milan have noted his progress and United will face a fight to hang on to the precocious winger.

Giggs' Welsh international team-mate has no doubt where the youngster is heading. "He has the ability to become one of the greatest players in the world."

Few people would argue with that.

RYAN GIGGS

Anfield

Graeme Souness is living on borrowed time at Liverpool. And unless he sorts out the Anfield mess this time it is almost certain to be his last season at the club.

Souness only just survived by the skin of his teeth after a disastrous 1992-93 season, rejecting the club's offer to pay up the remaining three years of his contract.

But it is that very determination to get things right which could yet see Souness guide Liverpool back to the heights of excellence they touched when he was their midfield inspiration during the mid-1980s.

Little has gone right for Souness since he succeeded Kenny Dalglish as Anfield boss in March, 1991.

Health problems have hardly helped the hard-as-nails Liverpool boss while his record in the transfer market has been little short of disastrous.

One look at Souness' signings (see table) during his first two years in charge show just why the Liverpool fans fear that he will never be the right man for the job.

THE SOUNESS SIGNINGS

Player	Fee	Hit/Miss
David James	£1.2m	MISS
Rob Jones	£300,000	HIT
Mark Wright	£2.2m	MISS
Torben Piechnik	£500,000	MISS
Stig-Inge Bjornebye	£600,000	MISS
Istvan Kozma	£300,000	MISS
Paul Stewart	£1.3m	MISS
Michael Thomas	£1.5m	MISS
Dean Saunders	£2.9m	MISS
Total	**£10.8m**	

Hardly inspiring, yet in fairness to the manager it has to be pointed out that precious few people complained at the time those deals were struck.

James, Wright, Stewart, Thomas and Saunders all failed to live up to expectations in a Liverpool shirt, though Souness hardly helped his cause by then gambling massively on untested Scandinavians Piechnik and Bjornebye.

Nor has the fact that Liverpool have had to spend £12 million on ground improvements at Anfield eased the situation. For whereas The Reds' reputation and resources once guaranteed them first option on every player who came onto the market, the club are now no better off than any one of ten of their Premier League rivals.

Yet it is not all gloom and doom at Anfield. And if anyone can save Souness it's the kids he has shown such faith in.

For while his no-nonsense style has upset established stars like Ian Rush, Bruce Grobbelaar and John Barnes, it has also earned him the unwavering loyalty of Jamie Redknapp, Rob Jones, Steve McManaman, Don Hutchison and Mike Marsh.

And it is those young talents who represent the future of a club in transition.

Face of the future - Don Hutchison

Face of the future - Rob Jones

Face of the future - Jamie Redknapp

Face of the future? Souness

Agony

But Souness can lift the Gloom

DECLINE & FALL
A season by season comparison of Liverpool's performances over the past 12 years.

Season	Lge.	FA Cup	Lge.Cup	Europe
1992-93	6th	3rd Rd	4th Rd	2nd Rd (CWC)
1991-92	6th	Winners	4th Rd	Q-F (UEFA)
1990-91	2nd	5th Rd	3rd Rd	
1989-90	1st	S-F	3rd Rd	
1988-89	2nd	Winners	4th Rd	
1987-88	1st	Finalists	3rd Rd	
1986-87	2nd	3rd Rd	Finalists	
1985-86	1st	Winners	S-F	
1984-85	2nd	S-F	3rd Rd	Final (EC)
1983-84	1st	4th Rd	Winners	Winners (EC)
1982-83	1st	5th Rd	Winners	Q-F (EC)
1981-82	1st	5th Rd	Winners	Q-F (EC)

CAN

ON A

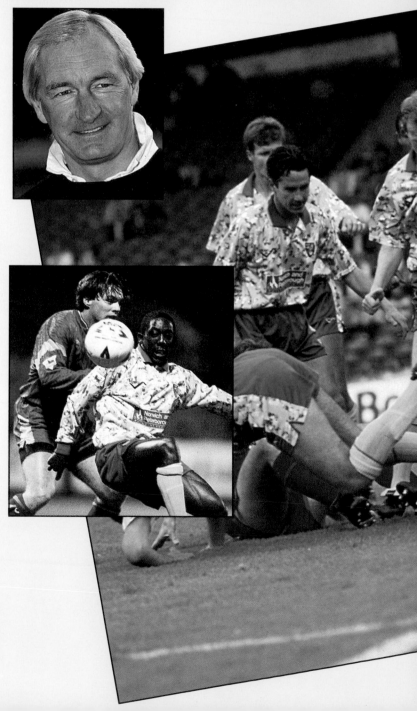

WHILE Jack Walker churns out cash like it's going out of fashion, and Manchester United, Aston Villa, Arsenal, Liverpool and the rest splash out millions to assemble Championship-chasing squads, one club has bucked the trend and built a successful side out of small change.

Norwich City's collection of has-beens, might-bes and never-weres rocked the Premier League last season - and they aim to keep on confounding the critics.

"We plan to be around for a few years yet," says manager Mike Walker. "A lot of people wrote us off last season, said we'd never stick the pace at the top.

"But I think we proved them wrong by staying towards the top of the table to the very end.

"Now I want to build on that success."

At the beginning of 1992-93, the Canaries were the bookies' favourites to fall off the Premier League perch and drop into Division One.

But their brand of fast, skilful football sent them into satellite, and made it a whole new ball game for the men from Carrow Road.

And their success brought financial rewards, as well as praise.

Admits Walker: "A lot of people have criticised Sky TV's involvement with the Premier League, but it's done the smaller clubs a big favour cash-wise.

"We were on telly nine or ten times last season, and also received a large sum for finishing third in the League.

"That sort of money can make or

ARIES
GOLDMINE

break a club like Norwich. I want to be able to look ahead and buy players - not worry about where the next quid's coming from."

Players like Dave Phillips, Bryan Gunn and Mark Robins became household names last season as Norwich defied the odds to go on winning.

But it hasn't all been goals and glory for The Canaries. As one of the top flight's smaller clubs they have to sell to survive - and that can wreck even the best laid plans.

You only need to look at the players Carrow Road has loved and lost to appreciate the task facing Mike Walker.

Stars like Chris Woods, Steve Bruce, Andy Townsend, Dale Gordon, Robert Fleck and Mike Phelan all mastered their art in the famous yellow and green before moving on to greater fame and fortune elsewhere.

"Managing a club like this involves a lot of hard work and being as shrewd as possible in the transfer market," claims Walker.

"We can't afford to fork out millions of pounds, so we have find younger players and bring through the system.

"The advantage is that we have a fantastic team spirit at Carrow Road - and that's a vital ingredient.

"But I would like to have some money to throw around to see what it's like!"

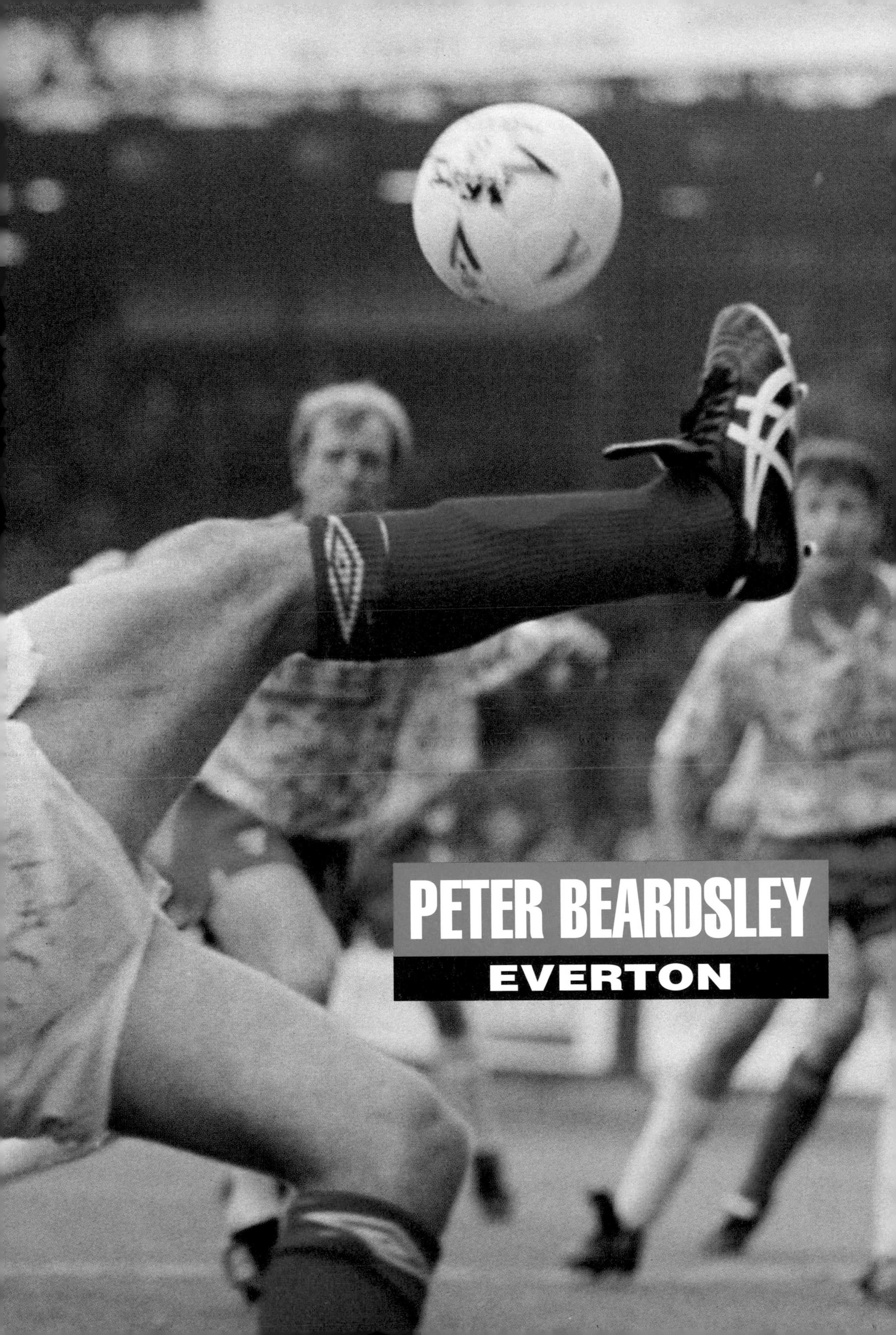
PETER BEARDSLEY
EVERTON

McCoist:
the dream
decade

ALLY McCOIST is celebrating ten glorious years at Ibrox and, virtually from day one, it's been goals all the way for the Scottish sensation.

"Coisty" revealed his goalscoring potential as a youngster with St. Johnstone and, after a disappointing spell at Sunderland, his talents have

reached fruition with Rangers.

During his dream decade as the darling of Ibrox he has picked up a constant stream of Championship and Cup-winners' medals — and a host of personal awards too.

Collecting the Shoot/Adidas Golden Boot as Scotland's leading scorer has become a way of life for Ally who has now plundered almost 300 League and Cup goals for the Glasgow giants.

Quite simply, there has been nobody to touch McCoist who, over the past ten years, has never failed to hit double figures and whose worst season's tally has been 18 goals.

The majority of strikers would settle for that total every year. Not Ally.

Goals are his lifeblood and the 300 he has scored for Rangers are one of the main reasons why the Ibrox outfit have become virtually invincible in recent times.

Star names, particularly during the Graeme Souness era, have come and gone but McCoist has remained loyal to the Light Blues.

ALLY McCOIST:

The Rangers Record Number of goals

Season	League	Cups	Europe	Total
1983-84	9	12	0	21
1984-85	12	5	1	18
1985-86	24	2	0	26
1986-87	33	2	2	37
1987-88	31	7	4	42
1988-89	9	9	0	18
1989-90	14	5	0	19
1990-91	11	4	3	18
1991-92	34	5	0	39
1992-93*	34	13	2	49
TOTALS:	**211**	**64**	**12**	**287**

figures correct up to end of 1992-93

READY

Rangers
& Scotland

10 things you dinnae ken about Ally McCOIST

1
● Alistair Murdoch McCoist was born at Bellshill Maternity Hospital on September 24, 1962. His star sign is Libra.

2
● Although he was a "wee laddy" at school his first position was centre-half. He also played at right-back and in midfield before finding his niche as a striker.

3
● He was brought up in East Kilbride and, apart from a brief spell with Sunderland, he has always lived within a few miles of the family home.

4
● His move to Sunderland was a disaster but one good thing to come out of it was that he met his wife Alison on Wearside.

5
● One of his few remaining ambitions as a player is to win the European Cup with Rangers.

6
● Ally is a dedicated follower of fashion and boasts an outrageous collection of hats, which earn him constant stick from his Rangers team-mates.

7
● He doesn't get much spare time but whenever he can he relaxes by listening to music — some of it is pretty heavy stuff too.

8
● His talents were not just confined to the playing field. He also passed eight O levels and two highers.

9
● He is the joker in the Rangers pack and something of a singing star at the club's end-of-season and Christmas parties.

10
● Ally's first winners' medal came in 1984 when he scored a hat-trick in the 3-2 win over Celtic in the League Cup Final.

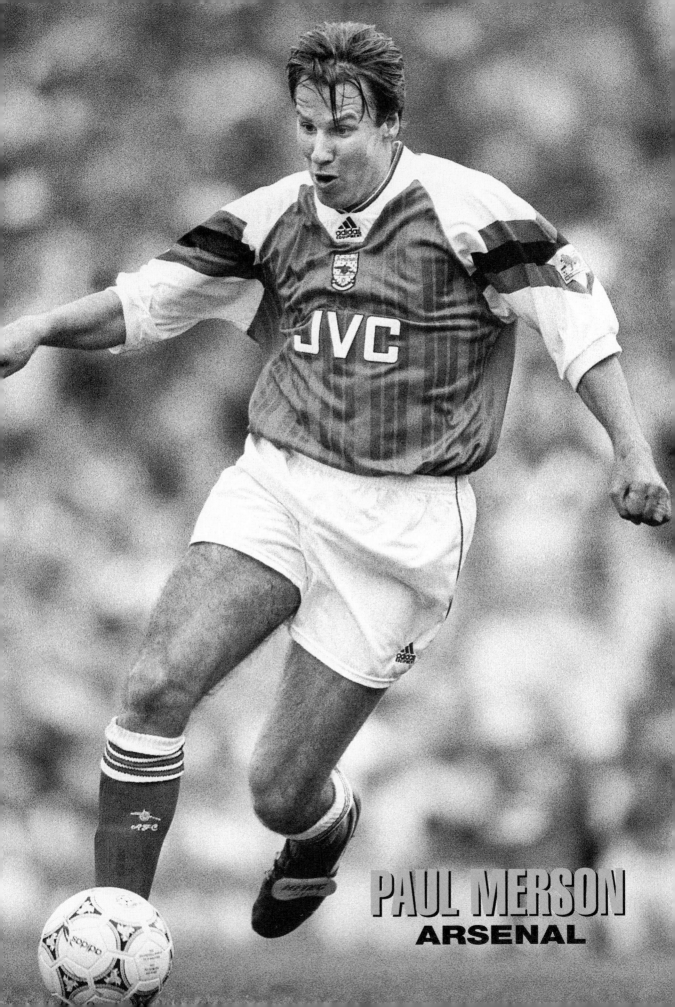

PAUL MERSON
ARSENAL

THE YORKSHIRE TERRIER

David Batty grew up as a Leeds fan and went on to skipper the side. Here's the story of one of Yorkshire's favourite sons.

DAVID was born in the Harehills area of Leeds on December 2nd 1968 and went to Brown Hill Primary School. His parents are Alan and Mary and almost as soon as he could walk the young David was being encouraged to kick a football.

While a seven-year-old pupil at Brown Hill Primary School David was taken to his first Leeds match.

It was in 1975 and Leeds were at home to Stoke.

"I remember standing on a box so that I could see. I was hooked from then on. All I ever wanted to do was play football," said David.

"I went to Shakespeare Middle School, Scott Hall Middle School and Allerton Grange High School. I wasn't bad at my school work, but I never considered any career other than

David Batty puts "Leeds before England"

football.

"My dad encouraged me all the way and has hardly ever missed a home match right from the time I first started playing for my school. He still keeps all my press cuttings and I know I can discuss things with him at any time and get some sensible advice. I owe him a great deal for all his help."

After playing for his school teams, David joined Leeds City Boys, a very strong local side. The next step was to

become a junior player with his beloved Leeds United.

"It was a dream just to be at the club and it still is. I wanted to be a Leeds player more than anything and I still can't believe that it has all come true."

Batty's progress through the juniors soon meant that he would be offered a fully professional contract and on July 3rd, 1987 he signed on the dotted line. As far as he was concerned, his

David's hero—Billy Bremner.

knew he would give you 100 per cent. He was well worth putting in the side even though he was only 18 at the time, as he has since proven."

It wasn't just at Leeds that David was grabbing attention. He also came under international scrutiny and was soon called up for England duty in the Under-18 side.

"We had some good matches. I remember the thrill of going to Brazil to play in a tournament. I'd like to go back there one day. it was quite a place and quite an experience."

His international career blossomed and on May 28th, 1988 he made his England Under-21 debut, coming on at half-time for Dennis Wise in a 1-1 draw against Switzerland in Lausanne.

The England goal was scored by a young lad from Newcastle by the name of Paul Gascoigne. In all David made seven appearances for the Under-21's and also played for the B team, but the chance of a full cap was his next dream. He didn't have to wait long.

"I got my first cap as substitute against the USSR at Wembley. I had been in the squad before, but that was the first time I got into a game. I was put on for Dennis Wise again. We won 3-1 and it was a real thrill."

England manager Graham Taylor saw enough to continue including Batty in his plans.

"I gave it some thought at the time and decided that the boy definitely had a future. He already had the ability to knit a team together and I knew that with more confidence and experience he could become out-standing," said the England manager.

One of the greatest points of being called up for England was that Batty had the chance to play alongside another of his heroes, Bryan Robson.

"I have always thought of him as a very good player, but it's not until you are in the same team that you realise

wildest dream had come true. But we now know that that was by no means the end of the story.

In November of that year he found himself on the team sheet of the first team and made his senior debut on November 21st, 1987 against Swindon. Leeds won 4-2.

"Billy Bremner was manager then and I have to say he was a great help to me in those early days. The former Leeds and Scotland skipper was already a hero to me and then when I found myself playing for him, well. You just had to try your hardest because you knew he always did."

If Batty was a fan of Bremner, the feeling was certainly mutual.

"You could see that David was a bit special," said Bremner.

"He had the right attitude and you

Leeds were worthy Champions in 1991-92.

David never shirks a challenge...as he proves here against Lawrie Sanchez of Wimbledon.

Hooked on Leeds... and fishing.

DAVID BATTY
(continued)

just how great he is. I like to think that we are similar players, but that doesn't mean that I consider myself to be as good as him. No way," said the Leeds star.

The local lad made good even more when he was picked to skipper the Leeds side, an honour which he always hoped for, but never truly expected to come his way.

"Football is all about dreams," said David.

"You dream of playing for your favourite club, you dream about playing for England. You dream about being captain of your team, You hope but you never really think it will happen to you. My dreams have come true so far so I think I'll dream about getting more goals!"

Batty has been handed the captain's armband several times when Gordon Strachan or Gary McAllister have been out of the side. One day he will probably be given the job permanently. His boss, Howard Wilkinson explains why.

"A captain has to be a good competitor, filled with an all-consuming desire to win. You can't be a

captain if you haven't got that. You can see that David has that character, a refusal to shirk responsibility and a hatred of losing any football match."

David does not dream about playing abroad. He doesn't even fancy leaving Leeds for another British club.

"I like it here. People say hello in the street, but in the right way. I'm Leeds born and bred. My fiancee, Mandy is from Leeds and my family and hers have known each other for years.

"Why should I ever think of leaving Leeds. The club is my second home. I come in on my days off because it means so much to me. I know everyone and have known most of them since I left school.

"If I ever had to choose between my club or my country, it would always be an easy win for Leeds. Elland Road is my life. I came here for the first time when I was seven and I shall still be coming here when I am 77.

"As far as I am concerned, the David Batty story begins and ends with Leeds United and that's fine by me."

ALAN SHEARER
BLACKBURN

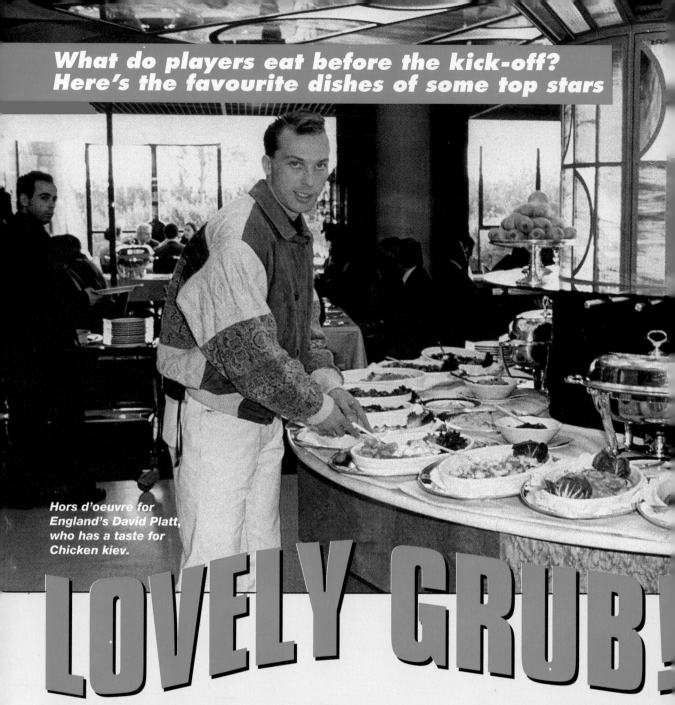

Hors d'oeuvre for England's David Platt, who has a taste for Chicken kiev.

LOVELY GRUB!

IMAGINE eating half a melon followed by steak and chips with all the trimmings, a giant bowl of ice cream and some cheese and biscuits swilled down with a pint of something or other and then going out to play 90 minutes of all-action Premier League soccer against Sheffield Wednesday.

Feeling sick? You would be, that's why players have only the lightest snack before a match although some of them like to pig-out at other times as we have discovered.

Beans on toast, some soup or scrambled egg used to be the favourite pre-match snack for most players and still is for many. But a lot of players have listened to the diet experts and go for something a little more exciting.

Darren Anderton could not be said to be less than energetic during a game and yet his favourite bite before a game is definitely not beans on toast.

"I like some roast chicken best of all. I like chicken at any time but before a match I like some because it is light and tasty yet you feel like you have had something worth having," said Darren.

Aston Villa's Tony Daley nods in agreement: "I like roast chicken for lunch."

Steve McManaman is also a chicken lover.

"Before a game I like to have a chicken omelette," said the Liverpool star who quickly added: "The day before a game I like to have a steak though — that's my favourite food."

Of course, favourite foods take us on to a different subject, but still one the stars enjoy talking about and mentioning steak, you'll find Manchester United skipper Steve Bruce head of the queue.

"I love a nice steak with a side salad and the whole works. It's always my first choice when we go out for a meal but, of course, I have something a lot lighter before a game. After a game it's a different matter — that's when I head for the steak house."

Soccer stars won't just eat anything that's thrust on the table. A lot have their dislikes, some quite surprising.

Nottingham Forest and England skipper Stuart Pearce is very definite about the grub he hates the most.

"Vegetables! I never liked them and

Pasta person Lee Martin.

more meal of the same carbohydrate foods and then they can eat what they like until two days before the next match."

Wise words indeed. Problem is that with most players now in action twice a week it doesn't leave a lot of time for eating what they like. But Professor Reilly's advice is still music to the ears of some players, especially the pasta freaks.

Manchester City player-manager Peter Reid is quite happy about that diet.

"I'm delighted to eat pasta and lots of it. I love the stuff and it doesn't bother me to stick to a pasta diet. Mind you, I have one ambition for when I stop playing — I want to get fat!"

Contrary to rumour, Rangers and Scotland star striker Ally McCoist is not a haggis addict. "I'm a pasta man. I don't mind having a lager with it to help it on its way although some mineral water does before a game."

Manchester United's Lee Martin is also into pasta in a big way.

"I think I had pasta before the FA Cup Final when I scored that winning goal against Crystal Palace. A lot happened that day so it's difficult to remember everything but I'm certainly a pasta person now."

Leeds and England defender Tony Dorigo also subscribes to the pasta club. "Yes, I like pasta a lot — I don't know what it does to improve my game but I like it because you can have so many different tastes with it and you don't feel bloated after-wards."

But fellow England star, Arsenal ace Ian Wright, has a different view.

Pasta time

"Pasta! Yuk! I can't stand it. I know it might be good for you but I just don't like it. You can have my share of pasta any time." Okay Ian, pasta plate.

Coventry scoring machine Mick Quinn is another pasta fan while Newcastle's Gavin Peacock likes anything Italian.

"I like Italian food a lot. I'm also learning Italian by the way, but it's not because I'm planning on joining an Italian club, honest. Honest! I like rice as well, but I'm not expecting to play in China!"

Spurs star Gary Mabbutt doesn't mind what he eats which is just as well because he does most of his own cooking. "I have a television perma-nently in the kitchen so that I can

watch something while I'm preparing my meal."

Aston Villa sensation Dean Saunders has also been known to turn his hand to the kitchen.

"I don't do a bad spaghetti bolognaise — and I don't mean out of a tin," said Dean. Wouldn't be a lot of use him cooking a meal for Lee Sharpe though.

"I like simple food. I don't really like anything spicy," Lee explained. Nigel Jemson shares his view. "I especially don't like Chinese food," said Nigel.

A lot of players enjoy fish. United's Micky Phelan is a fish fan and Scottish star Charlie Nicholas tells us he loves salmon. Gary Speed of Leeds and Wales doesn't agree. "I don't mind fish and chips, but the idea of eating raw fish makes me want to throw up," said Gary.

Talking of throwing up, Derby's England Under-21 forward Tommy Johnson has no trouble remembering what he hated the most.

"Snails! Horrible. I tried them once — never again," said Tommy.

David Platt hasn't gained much of a taste for Italian food — he still rates Chicken Kiev as his favourite dish. Paul Ince has a similarly exotic taste in food.

Banana king

"I like McDonalds best," said Paul. The lads at Coventry will agree with him — their boss Bobby Gould is forever heading for the nearest McDonalds after a match.

But perhaps we should return to fitness food and spare a thought for Lesley Strachan, long suffering wife of Gordon O.B.E. (not One Boiled Egg). Seaweed is one of Gordon's delights and of course, he is famous for his love of bananas. Nearly every morning Lesley prepares his breakfast of Scottish porridge (it must be the real stuff) with no sugar or salt, but with sliced banana and a mug of orange juice.

"People might find that a bit disgusting," Gordon admitted. "You get the best from the carbohydrates of the porridge and the best minerals and vitamins from the bananas, so I thought I'd just shove them in together. It fills me up and I don't need much at lunchtime. The seaweed is in table form.

"Sunday is the day when the rubbish comes out. Bacon, sausages, eggs, the whole lot. But it's all grilled and the eggs are poached. On the night before a match I make sure I have pasta."

Oh no, not pasta again! Is it really that important?

"There's no magic diet, you should just be sensible with what you eat," said Gordon.

So really when it comes to choosing food for fitness, you just have to use your loaf!

I don't suppose I ever will. They are very boring. I like something a bit more interesting?" said Stuart. Bet he enjoys a plate of chips though.

But he's not alone in his dislike of the veg even if mums still insist that we all eat our "greens". Matthew Le Tissier doesn't hesitate when asked what food makes him grumpy — "Vegetables, I just don't like them," he said.

What you eat is more important than many people realise. Everton called in sports fitness expert Tommy Reilly a couple of years ago to sort out the diets of their stars.

"We have proved that a high carbohydrate diet for two days prior to a game is beneficial," said Professor Reilly.

"Pasta, cannelloni, spaghetti (but no pizzas) are fine. Also bread, rice, cereals, boiled or jacket potatoes, but no milk, butter, cheese, fish or steaks should be taken. Plenty of fruit is good, especially bananas.

"This type of food provides muscle energy for long periods. After the game the players should have one

SPALL

ROMAN GLASS

Buketa

DAGENHAM MOTORS

BILLY'S BOYS WON'T GO DOWN

TOO GOOD for the First Division - not good enough for the Premier League.

That's been West Ham's dilemma for the past few years as Billy Bonds' team of entertainers have bounced from promotion to relegation and back again in successive seasons.

Now The Hammers are determined to prove they can live with the big boys after last term's dramatic promotion success, when they snatched second place away from Portsmouth on the final day thanks to just one more goal scored.

Not that anybody at Upton Park is believes it's going to be easy.

Bonds set the tone for the current campaign the minute that promotion was sealed when he announced: "The Premier League is broken into three categories - the teams challenging for the Championship, the mid-table teams and the teams battling to beat the drop. Our aim is to finish top of that third group."

It's not surprising that Bonds is looking enviously at fellow promotion winners Newcastle, who have spent extensively to strengthen their squad.

For instead of making new signings, Bonds has actually been ordered to cut his squad by eight players in order to reduce an annual wage bill of £2.6 million which was swallowing two-thirds of the club's gate receipts.

Even so, Bonds is still confident of his team giving a better account of themselves than they managed in 1991-92, when they finished bottom of the old First Division with just 38 points from 42 games.

"We might not have any money in the bank, but we are rich in spirit," insists Bonds. "And that counts for a hell of a lot."

Nobody typifies that fighting spirit better than full-back Julian Dicks (right), whose disciplinary problems have overshadowed the fact that there is no better left-back in the country.

In fact it's that added steel in West Ham's play which could just prove their salvation this season.

In previous years their stylish approach play was often betrayed by a soft centre.

Now they have Dicks, Martin Allen, Tim Breacker and Peter Butler providing the bite to back up the proven goalscoring potential of Trevor Morley and Clive Allen.

And though many Hammers fans fear the worst, former Upton Park star Jimmy Greaves takes a more optimistic approach.

"Everyone says Newcastle will take the Premier by storm while West Ham will go straight back down, but I don't think there's all that much between them," says Greavsie.

"OK, so they're not the greatest team in the world at the moment, but neither are most of the other teams in the Premier League.

"Take away the top four or five teams and any of the other teams have as much chance of finishing in the top ten as the bottom three.

"If they can finish mid-table this season and make a bit of money from the TV deal, they'll be in a much stronger position to do something more spectacular next time out."

DARREN ANDERTON
TOTTENHAM

HAVE you got your bucket and spade with you? We're off to the seaside.
Actually, you might be better off to bring a football with you because we're
going on a tour of the British coast, to find the clubs who like to be beside the
seaside so much that they actually live there. Whether you are on holiday or
just visiting for the day or weekend, why not take the chance to check out the
clubs who love the sea, sand and air of our most popular resorts.

Football took pride of place from rugby in Plymouth

BLACKPOOL

You can find their ground in
Bloomfield Road and the club shop
is open most days from 9am to 5pm.
The club was founded in 1887 by
old boys of St. John's School. Their
first League match was on
September 5th, 1896 when they lost
1-3 to Lincoln.
Ground capacity: 10,337.
Record attendance: 38,098 v
Wolves, Division One, 1955.
Pitch size: 111 yards x 73 yards.
Nickname: The Seasiders.

BOURNEMOUTH

Their home is Dean Court and their
club shop is open from 9am-5pm
daily. There used to be a club called
Boscombe St. John's Club, but a
meeting in a house in Gladstone
Road led to the birth of Bournemouth
in 1899. Their first League match
was on August 25th, 1923 when they
lost 1-3 to Swindon.
Ground capacity: 11,428.
Record attendance: 28,799 v
Manchester United, FA Cup, 1957.
Pitch size: 112 yards x 75 yards.
Nickname: The Cherries.

BRIGHTON

You can find their ground in neighbouring Hove,
and the Goldstone Ground is on Old Shoreham
Road. The club shop is usually only open on
match days but a phone call to 0273 26412 will
do the trick if you want it open. The club was
started by a group of Scotsmen, but was
disbanded two seasons later. Manager John
Jackson wanted to keep top soccer alive in the
area and formed the new club in 1900. Their
first League match was on August 28th, 1920
when they lost 0-2 to Southend.
Ground capacity: 18,647.
Record attendance: 36,747 v Fulham, Division
Two, 1958.
Pitch size: 112 yards x 75 yards.
Nickname: The Seagulls.

SOUTHAMPTON

Take a trip down Milton Road to find The Dell. The club shop is open daily from 9am to 5pm. The club was formed from Deanery FC, mostly school teachers who were associated with St. Mary's Church. What an appropriate nickname they have! They started in 1885 and their first League match came on August 28th, 1920 when they drew 1-1 with Gillingham.
Ground capacity: 21,900.
Record attendance: 31,044 v Manchester United, Division One, 1969.
Pitch size: 110 yards x 72 yards.
Nickname: The Saints.

SOUTHEND

Southend Athletic was a crack amateur side, but today's club was formed almost in opposition and was very ambitious, turning professional straight away in 1906. Their first League match, like many others, was on August 28th, 1920. They beat Brighton 2-0. The Roots Hall ground can be found on Victoria Avenue and the club shop is open each day, except Wednesdays, from 10.30am to 4.30pm.
Ground capacity: 14,428.
Record attendance: 31,090 v Liverpool, FA Cup, 1979.
Pitch size: 110 yards x 74 yards
Nickname: The Shrimpers or Blues.

Continued over

GRIMSBY TOWN

Their Blundell Park ground is actually in the resort of Cleethorpes just off the Grimsby Road. The club shop is open from 10am to 4pm most days. Grimsby were founded in 1878 as Grimsby Pelham FC after a meeting at the Wellington Arms pub which is still in Freeman Street, Grimsby. The Pelham part is the name of landowners in the area. Their first League match was on September 3rd, 1892 when they beat Northwich Victoria 2-1.
Ground capacity: 17,526.
Record attendance: 31,651 v Wolves, FA Cup, 1937.
Pitch size: 111 yards x 74 yards.
Nickname: The Mariners.

PORTSMOUTH

Fratton Park can be found on Frogmore Road and the club shop is open each weekday from 9am to 5pm. Alderman J.E. Pink, a solicitor, called together five other businessmen and they decided to buy a piece of land near Goldsmith Avenue for £4,950. That was in 1898 and they quickly developed it as a football stadium and brought in the players to give the club a flying start. Their first League match was on August 28th, 1920 and they beat Swansea 3-0.
Ground capacity: 26,352.
Record attendance: 51,385 v Derby, FA Cup, 1949.
Pitch size: 116 yards x 73 yards.
Nickname: Pompey.

PLYMOUTH

Their stadium is in the lovely Home Park and their club shop is open daily from 9am to 5pm. Plymouth was once a rugby stronghold, but a number of servicemen preferred soccer. A meeting at Argyle Terrace, Mutley in 1886 led to Argyle Athletic Club being formed to play both sports. The rugby team later disbanded and the soccer team went from strength to strength. Their first League match was on August 28th, 1920 when they drew 1-1 with Norwich.
Ground capacity: 19,700.
Record attendance: 43,596 v Aston Villa, Division Two, 1936.
Pitch size: 112 yards x 75 yards.
Nickname: The Pilgrims.

SCARBOROUGH

The McCain Stadium proudly stands on the Seamer Road. The club shop is open from 9.30am to 5pm on weekdays and until noon on Saturdays. The club was formed in 1879 by cricketers and they played on the North Marine Road Cricket Ground in those days. More than 100 years later they played their first League match on August 15th, 1987 when they drew 2-2 with Wolves.
Ground capacity: 7,176.
Record attendance: 11,130 v Luton, FA Cup, 1938.
Pitch size: 120 yards x 75 yards.
Nickname: Boro.

The sea air didn't do Sunderland much good last season.

Aberdeen are gunning for Rangers

SUNDERLAND

There are some nice beaches at Sunderland and the ground is not far from them in Grantham Road. That's where you'll find the famous Roker Park. The club shop is open from 9am to 5pm from Monday to Saturday. This is another club formed by teachers in 1879 and originally called the Sunderland and District Teachers Association Football Club. What a mouthful! No wonder they ran into financial problems and had to call in outsiders and turn into plain Sunderland. Their first League match was on September 13th, 1890 when they lost 2-3 to Burnley.
Ground capacity: 31,887.
Record attendance: 75,118 v Derby, FA Cup, 1933.
Pitch size: 113 yards x 74 yards.
Nickname: The Rokermen.

SCOTLAND

What if you're going to Scotland? Well, there are some seaside clubs there, too.

ABERDEEN

Ground: Pittodrie Stadium, Pittodrie Street.
Founded: 1903.
Joined League: 1904.
Nickname: The Dons.
Pitch size: 110 yards x 72 yards.
Ground capacity: 21,779.
Record attendance: 45,061 v Hearts, Scottish Cup, 1954.

ARBROATH

Ground: Gayfield Park.
Founded: 1878.
Joined League: 1902.
Nickname: The Red Lichties.
Pitch size: 115 yards x 71 yards.
Ground capacity: 7,000.
Record attendance: 13,510 v Rangers, Scottish Cup, 1952.

Gayfield Park, Arbroath is about as close as you can get to the sea

AYR

Ground: Somerset Park, Tryfield Place.
Founded: 1910.
Joined League: 1910.
Nickname: The Honest Men.
Pitch size: 111 yards x 72 yards.
Ground capacity: 15,870.
Record attendance: 25,225 v Rangers, Division One, 1969.

BERWICK RANGERS

Ground: Shielfield Park, Tweedmouth.
Founded: 1881.
Joined League: 1935.
Nickname: The Borderers.
Pitch size: 112 yards x 76 yards.
Ground capacity: 5,235.
Record attendance: 13,365 v Rangers, Scottish Cup, 1967.

MONTROSE

Ground: Links Park, Wellington Street.
Founded: 1879.
Joined League: 1929.
Nickname: The Gable Endies.
Pitch size: 113 yards x 70 yards.
Ground capacity: 6,500.
Record attendance: 8,983 v Dundee, Scottish Cup, 1973.

RAITH ROVERS

Ground: Stark's Park, Pratt Street, Kirkcaldy.
Founded: 1883.
Joined League: 1902.
Nickname: Rovers.
Pitch size: 113 yards x 67 yards.
Ground capacity: 8,500.
Record attendance: 31,306 v Hearts, Scottish Cup, 1953.

Now it's your turn!

All you have to do is find the clubs on the map of Britain. Check on page 125 to see if you got them all right.

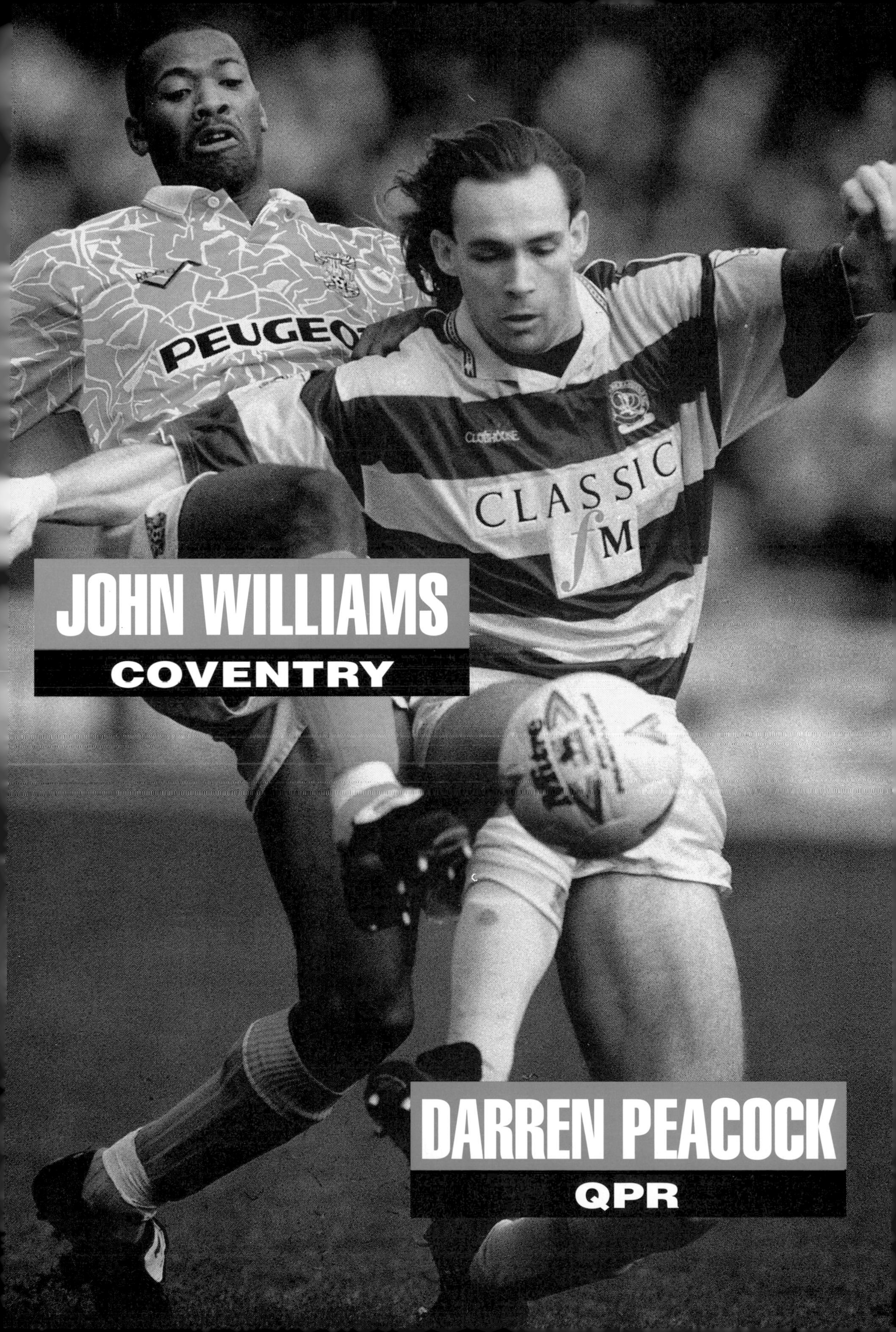

JOHN WILLIAMS
COVENTRY

DARREN PEACOCK
QPR

YOU WON'T BELIEVE IT
but it's true!

Groan goal!

● ALAN MULLERY has a record he would rather forget. When he was playing for Fulham against Sheffield Wednesday in a League match on January 21st, 1961, he passed back to his goalkeeper seconds after the kick-off and the ball went straight into his own goal. Not only is that the fastest own goal on record, but Wednesday were ahead without even touching the ball!

Unlucky 13

● MANCHESTER UNITED are one of the biggest crowd-pullers in the game yet in 1921 only 13 people turned up for a League match at Old Trafford. It isn't quite what it seems though, for the game was actually a Second Division match between Stockport and Leicester and was played at Old Trafford because Stockport's ground was closed by the Football Association.

Mum's the word

● LEEDS and Wales star Gary Speed is the pride of his mum since he made it all the way to the top in soccer, but there was a time she tried to talk him out of it. Gary played cricket for Wales as a schoolboy and his mother thought that he could make a career in cricket. That's why she tried to talk him out of concentrating on soccer.

Rich man?

● HOW times change. When Pele was probably at his peak in the early 1960's he was officially earning twice as much as the President of Brazil. Pele's club, Santos, were paying him £300 per month! With bonuses he was actually getting about £1,000 a week and was the world's richest footballer. Knowing that some of today's international stars are earning more than that every day, what would Pele be worth now?

Record "breaker"

● BRYAN ROBSON'S list of injuries could fill a medical dictionary, but his worst spell must still be during the 1976-77 season when he was playing — sort of — for West Brom. On October 2nd of that season he broke a leg playing against Spurs. After eight weeks he was back in action, but broke a leg again having a run out with the reserves against Stoke. He fought back to the first team and on April 16th broke it for the third time in six months when playing against Manchester City. It's a hat-trick that still makes Bryan wince.

Ref in a knot!

● WHO would be a referee? They come in for all sorts of abuse. One poor ref found that his job had strings attached when he took charge of the match between Racing Cruz and Estoril Mendoza in Argentina. A fan, annoyed at the ref's decisions, ran on to the pitch with a rope, lassoed the ref and tied him up while telling him what he though of him. It took the police ten minutes to release the unhappy man in the middle.

Humble Gunner

● ARSENAL have one of the finest grounds in Europe, but it wasn't always like that. Their first grandstand at Plumstead was a line of army wagons. The man at the turnstile was David Danskin, who was also skipper of the side. He used to take the money until it was kick-off time and then lead his side out for the match. Imagine Tony Adams doing that.

High grounds

● The Hawthorns, home of West Bromwich Albion is the highest ground in English soccer in that it is 541 feet above sea level. That's nothing compared with some of the grounds used during the Mexico World Cup. Mexico City's famous Azteca Stadium is about 7,000 feet above sea level.

Scoring keeper

● DID you hear about the goalkeeper who scored on his debut? Yes, it did happen and it wasn't an own goal. Belgian-born Mark De Clerek made his debut for Aberdeen on August 31st, 1980, playing against Berwick Rangers in the Scottish League Cup. He booted a long clearance and it went straight up the field and into Berwick's goal!

Best's UK tour

● GEORGE BEST once played in all four Home countries in senior matches in a space of ten days. It started when he played for Northern Ireland against Iceland in Belfast on September 21st, 1977. Three days later he was playing for Fulham away to Cardiff and then on September 26th he was again playing for Fulham at St. Mirren in an Anglo-Scottish Cup match and rounded off his unique tour by being in the Fulham side that played at Crystal Palace on October 1st. While we're on the subject, how about that for fixture congestion?

Head case

● SOCCER daft Aaron Benwell, aged 12, was suspended from Rushcliffe comprehensive school in Nottingham because he had the name of his favourite player shaved into his hair. Aaron was proud to carry Des Walker around on his head. "I think he is a great footballer", said Aaron. Good job he isn't a fan of Alexei Mikhailichenko!

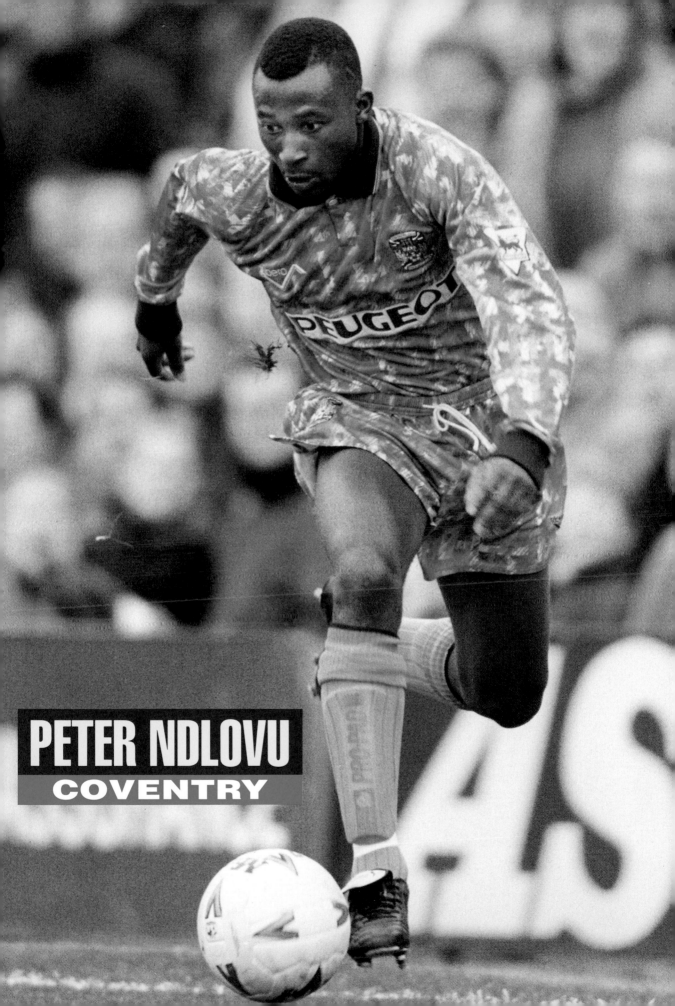

PETER NDLOVU
COVENTRY

PREMIER PRIZE!

YOU need a team of Supermen and a captain fed on spinach to give him Popeye-like strength to win the Premier League Championship.

Come the day when the boys collect their prize - that gleaming 30 inch trophy - all the skipper's extra weight-lifting exercises will be needed to haul the 23lb prize above his head.

And so it was with Steve Bruce of Manchester United, who became the first player to get his hands on the new Premier League trophy.

Almost the same amount of blood, sweat and tears had come into the winning of the trophy as had been involved in creating it.

The story began last summer when Garrods, the Royal jewellers, approached the Football Association about the new trophy.

Trevor Brown, Garrods' head designer, came up with six models which fulfilled an initial brief for an "English" looking trophy with two handles and a lid.

Steve Sanson, the Garrods spokesman, said: "It is a very classical-style cup. The Greek urn shape makes it look simple yet imposing and the crown lid and lions give the trophy its identity.

"Although the crown and lions are gold they are in fact solid silver, plated with gold. The trophy is made of sterling silver."

Garrods, who have made the America's Cup yachting trophy, almost all the golf cups in circulation and the Texaco Trophy cricket prize, took ten weeks to make the trophy once the designs were agreed.

LEE RICHARDSON

ABERDEEN

Keegan
Geordie

HE CAME, he saw, he conquered - twice! Kevin Keegan has twice proved to be the hero of St. James's Park. The first time was as a player, but perhaps this time has been even more amazing because when Keegan arrived back on Tyneside he began the great NEWCASTLE REVOLUTION.

IT was Keegan the soccer superstar, the former England skipper who first pulled on a Newcastle shirt after a surprise transfer from Southampton. Manager Arthur Cox was determined to get his Magpies into Division One and he succeeded.

In two seasons Keegan scored 48 goals in 78 League games. He became a superhero in Newcastle and there were more than a few grown men crying when he announced his retirement and actually bowed out after a friendly with Liverpool, making his exit in true Keegan style - in a helicopter.

Kevin said at the time that he was finishing with football and indeed little was heard of him for some time. But plenty was heard of Newcastle as they slumped from the stuff dreams are made of into the depths of despair.

Manager Arthur Cox got fed up and went to Derby. Jack Charlton took over for a few months and then Willie McFaul gave it his best shot for three years.

Experienced Jim Smith had a go for a couple of seasons before

n's Dreamland

Keegan and Hall - the dynamic duo

announcing that he believed the club was unmanageable. Ossie Ardiles followed him in and pleased the fans, but not his bosses.

Less than 72 hours after getting the dreaded vote of confidence from the board, Ossie was sacked and the whole turmoil of boardroom battles, a very real threat of relegation to Division Three and unhappy fans rushed to the fore.

Within hours there was a new sensation as Kevin Keegan was named as the new manager of Newcastle United.

Magpies fans will never forget February 5th, 1992, and why should they? It was the start of their revolution. Sir John Hall had taken a controlling interest in the ailing club and not only eased the debts but was prepared to inject some much-needed cash to make Newcastle great again just as it had been in the past when the League title was won four times and the FA Cup six times.

"It really was the only job in football

that I wanted," said Kevin. "I would not have come back into the game for anything else. I saw Newcastle as having the greatest potential of any club in Britain. And I still believe that."

At the time of stepping into the management hot seat Keegan vowed to revive Newcastle's glorious past.

"I'm so excited. I can't tell you how much. This is the most exciting thing that has ever happened to me in my life."

He immediately appointed former Liverpool team-mate Terry McDermott as his assistant and then the work started.

There was the battle against relegation to fight first and the new Kev and Terry show got rolling. One of the first to wish them success was Ossie Ardiles.

Not far behind him was Kev's old boss Lawrie McMenemey, who said that Keegan was the perfect choice for the job and that Newcastle's troubles would soon be over.

Lawrie was right, of course, but there were still some hiccups on the road to success. Keegan's first match in charge was at home to Bristol City. Nearly 30,000 fans turned up to welcome him home and the party went into overdrive at the final whistle when the Magpies had won 3-0 and moved one place up the table to 22nd.

The remaining matches of the season included a run of defeats, but nobody cared when Newcastle's safety was finally assured.

Lee Clark is one of Newcastle's brightest stars

with new loan signing Dave Beasant, himself a former Magpie, making his debut, earned a 1-0 win to take the pressure off.

The Keegan improvement scheme has not yet finished. Sir. John Hall is prepared to put up more cash to help Newcastle achieve their ultimate - a place among Europe's elite.

"My ultimate aim is for Newcastle to become a major force in British football," said Sir John. "We have the fans and the potential. We are on our way and we are in a hurry. I want to see us at the very top within three years and then I want us to be successful in Europe."

Quite how the likes of Jean-Pierre Papin and Marco Van Basten would react to the unique atmosphere of St James's Park is anybody's guess, but it would certainly be a culture shock for them.

The glory days are, without doubt, on their way back to Newcastle and it seems only a matter of time before the club is again challenging for the game's major honours.

And King Kevin is quick to praise the part the supporters have played in the club's recent successes.

"I can't say enough about the fans," said Keegan. "They are sensational. Every new player who comes here is amazed by them. I want success for them because they really deserve it - they are incredible."

There were only thoughts now for the future.

There was a heart-stopping moment for Magpies fans when it was announced that Keegan and McDermott had walked out on the club after a cash with the chairman.

"I felt at the time that promises I had received weren't being kept and that was affecting our chances of being successful," recalled Keegan. "But that's all water under the bridge now. It was sorted out quite quickly and we are all united now."

Keegan inherited some great players like Lee Clark and Gavin Peacock, but he added to his talented crew by spending wisely.

Barry Venison was bought from Liverpool. Portsmouth defender John Beresford was signed after Liverpool turned him down on

medical grounds. Robert Lee was talked into leaving his beloved Charlton to sign for the Magpies and Brian Kilcline joined from Oldham. Andy Cole cost £1.75 million from Bristol City and became the club's record signing.

Together they have combined well to get Newcastle on the road to the top. Along the way, Keegan has had even greater ambitions to sign some of soccer's supernames. Stars like Chris Waddle, Mark Hughes, Peter Beardsley and even Dean Saunders are among those that Keegan has tried to buy.

At the start of the season Newcastle got off to a flying star that kept them at the top throughout the campaign. They won each of their first ten League matches, a run that only came to a halt when Grimsby Town,

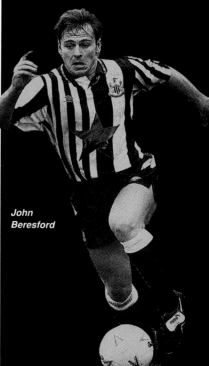

John Beresford

PAUL WALSH
PORTSMOUTH

QUIZ SOCCER

How good is your geography?

Can you name the countries where these clubs are based?

1. Neuchatel (right)
2. Apoel
3. Ferencvaros
4. Drogheda
5. Auxerre
6. Anderlecht
7. Eintracht
8. Lyngby
9. FC Twente
10. Zaragoza

How good is your history?

In which years did these events take place?

1. In which year did Liverpool first win the European Cup (right)?
2. When did Spurs last win the UEFA Cup?
3. In which year was the first World Cup?
4. Celtic were the first British team to win the European Cup, but when?

5. When was the first FA Cup Final at Wembley?
6. In which year did Peter Shilton (left) retire from international soccer?
7. The FA was founded when?
8. In which year did Brian Clough become manager of Nottingham Forest?
9. Ryan Giggs (above) was born in which year?
10. In which year did England win the World Cup?

How good is your maths?

So you think you are good with sums eh? Try your hand at these.

1. How much did Lazio pay Spurs for Gazza?
2. If a team wins three and draws two of its last eight Premier League games, how many points has it dropped?

SCHOOL TIME

AND NOW IT'S PLAY-TIME

Which Notts County footballer sits on top of a cake?

Which Arsenal player likes boats?

Which Villa player trains seven times a week?

Which Chelsea player isn't silly?

Which Wednesday player isn't dull?

Which Leeds player isn't the slowest?

Which Manchester United player pierces defences?

Which Premier League 'keeper is the pick of the bunch?

Which Newcastle star was dear to buy?

Which manager has the biggest job in Leicester?

Why does Father Christmas like to wear a No. 9 soccer shirt? . . . Because he's a Santa Forward!

Why did Mark Hateley wear swimming trunks? . . . So that he could do diving headers!

Why does Vinny Jones carry a felt tip pen on the pitch? . . . So that he can mark the opposition!

Why does Les Ferdinand take lessons from Paul Daniels? . . . So that he can do a hat-trick!

What's black and white and goes under water? . . . One of Kevin Keegan's Newcastle subs!

Answers on page 115

---

3. How many goals were scored in the 1966 World Cup Final?

4. What was the capacity of Wembley before it was all-seater?

5. How many full England caps did Bobby Moore (right) win?

6. How many players are named for a Football League match?

7. How many yellow cards is a player shown before being sent-off?

8. How much did Middlesbrough pay Sunderland for Alf Common in 1905?

9. How many teams were relegated from Division Two last season?

10. How many goals did striker Bobby Charlton score for England?

SKATING OI

IT WAS a bleak winter in 1963 and snow and ice caused havoc in the soccer season. In fact the 1962-63 campaign broke all previous records for postponements due to bad weather.

More than 400 League and Cup games were hit by the weather during a six week spell early in 1963 and on February 9th only seven matches were completed in the whole of Britain. But for one enterprising club it was not such bad news.

Of all people, it was **HALIFAX TOWN** who took advantage of the freeze-up.

They were the first club in the country to benefit from the bad weather by opening up their pitch as a skating rink.

The ice was thick enough and Halifax simply played pop music over their sound system and charged people 2s 6d (13p) to skate. Hundreds of people who had never been near the ground before turned up to have some fun on the ice.

The Halifax ground was also peculiar because it was the home of the local speedway team, the track running around the perimeter of the pitch. There used to be quite a few grounds which also had speedway or greyhound racing tracks around them — Wembley still does.

In Scotland, **COWDENBEATH** used to have soccer in the afternoons and stock car racing in the evenings on the same day which meant that the ground was always busy. But the tales of other sports at grounds are nothing compared with some of the odd stories surrounding some of our best known stadia.

At **HIGHBURY**, there is a horse buried. The unfortunate horse died when it fell into a hole while delivering rubble to help create Arsenal's famous North Bank terraces. It was left in the hole and has certainly witnessed some great days with The Gunners.

Horses have a connection with **LIVERPOOL**, too. The famous Kop flagpole is a mast from an iron ship. It was erected at Anfield in 1928 after a team of horses dragged it from the docks. The Spion Kop, sadly now changed to suit the Taylor report, is named after a hill in South Africa

Amazing stories from around the grounds

where many Liverpudlians died during the Boer War in 1900.

Not to be outdone, rivals **EVERTON** have a quirky little tale in connection with Goodison. The Toffeemen have their own church in a corner of the ground. The church was there before the soccer club and whatever ground improvements are made, the church must stay.

When Everton put up their new stands, architects had to be careful not to design anything that harmed the church.

NORTHAMPTON'S County Ground (right) serves as a cricket ground as well as a soccer stadium. **SHEFFIELD UNITED** used to be the

THE PITCH

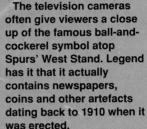

same. For more than 80 years The Blades used to have to time their early season fixtures so cricket could continue at Bramall Lane.

The old cricket pavilion finally disappeared during ground developments in 1973, a little ironic really since The Blades were only started because the cricket team wanted something to do during the winter.

Dave Bassett's men have another story about their ground — it was in 1985 when Oldham were to be visitors on February 9th. The match had to be postponed, but not because of the weather — a 2,000lb German bomb left over from World War II was discovered just outside the ground.

HULL CITY used to be one of the easiest clubs in the country to travel to since it had its own railway station at the ground. These days the remains of the station are still there but the trains thunder past to the city centre. Many fans would like to see a return to the days when "training" took on a different meaning at Boothferry Park.

NOTTINGHAM FOREST'S riverside City Ground might not have anything strange about it, but it has been the scene of some great soccer revolutions — and not just those involving Brian Clough.

Shinguards were worn there for the first time In 1874 by Forest's England international Sam Widdowson. Four years later a referee used a whistle for the first time, waving a handkerchief having been the previous way a ref signalled during a match.

Then in 1891 the crossbar and nets made their first appearance, again at the City Ground.

SHREWSBURY'S Gay Meadow (below) is also a riverside stadium. It is so close to the water that on match days the club has a boat on standby to fish the ball out of the river if it goes out of the ground.

Back in North London there is something of a legend about one of the famous landmarks at **WHITE HART LANE.**

The television cameras often give viewers a close up of the famous ball-and-cockerel symbol atop Spurs' West Stand. Legend has it that it actually contains newspapers, coins and other artefacts dating back to 1910 when it was erected.

WIMBLEDON'S old Plough Lane ground used to be a swamp and a rubbish dump — no wonder they wanted to move.

One of the best grounds in the country is **ELLAND ROAD** where Leeds have developed an old brickyard. Multi-million pound stands now tower over what was once a pile of rubble but there is one link with the past — a well.

It remains in a corner of the West Stand, but there is no truth in the rumour that manager Howard Wilkinson used to throw coins in it and make a wish last season.

All soccer roads lead to **WEMBLEY**, but they might have been leading somewhere entirely different but for a failed venture. An attempt was made to build a tower to rival the famous Eiffel Tower of Paris, but because of the ground conditions the project could not be safely completed.

Instead the area was scooped out and 250,000 tons of clay removed to start the building what has become the most famous soccer stadium in the world — a long way from Halifax.

We capture top stars enjoying themselves off the park ...

Leeds and England midfield star David Rocastle looks like he's having a splashing time

Right a bit, left a bit - fire - Vinny's nailed another opponent - and not a football in sight

We bet a few Scottish 'keepers wish Ally could be caged up on Saturday's afternoons

PLAYERS AT PLAY

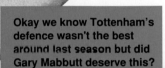

Okay we know Tottenham's defence wasn't the best around last season but did Gary Mabbutt deserve this?

It's not often that Les Ferdinand has to take a back seat - many say he's Simply the Best

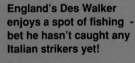

England's Des Walker enjoys a spot of fishing - bet he hasn't caught any Italian strikers yet!

Manchester City 'keeper Tony Coton keeps himself amused while he waits for his local to open

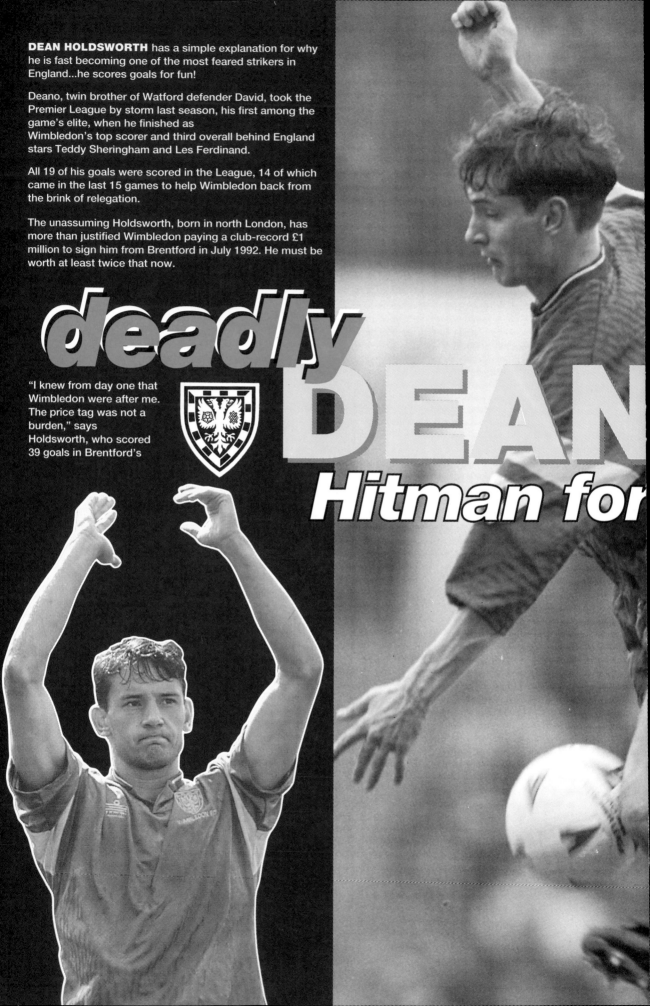

DEAN HOLDSWORTH has a simple explanation for why he is fast becoming one of the most feared strikers in England...he scores goals for fun!

Deano, twin brother of Watford defender David, took the Premier League by storm last season, his first among the game's elite, when he finished as Wimbledon's top scorer and third overall behind England stars Teddy Sheringham and Les Ferdinand.

All 19 of his goals were scored in the League, 14 of which came in the last 15 games to help Wimbledon back from the brink of relegation.

The unassuming Holdsworth, born in north London, has more than justified Wimbledon paying a club-record £1 million to sign him from Brentford in July 1992. He must be worth at least twice that now.

deadly DEAN

"I knew from day one that Wimbledon were after me. The price tag was not a burden," says Holdsworth, who scored 39 goals in Brentford's

Hitman for

the Crazy Gang!

1992 Third Division championship-winning season. "In fact it was most flattering.

"I'm just happy that I was able to pay back the faith manager Joe Kinnear and chairman Sam Hammam showed in me when I was struggling earlier in the season."

This type of support, according to Holdsworth, is one of the most endearing features of the South London club that is so often singled out for unwarranted criticism.

"I love Wimbledon even though we're often on a hiding to nothing. It's not in my nature to be extrovert but I do enjoy being part of the crazy gang.

"Everyone wants to be a rebel in life and we have 11 at this club."

The transition from Third Division to Premier League proved relatively smooth for Holdsworth.

"I like to think I took it in my stride. I enjoyed every game - even the ones we lost," he says.

"As a striker you are judged on goals and nothing else. If I hadn't scored many, people would have said I didn't fit in.

"The main difference is the overall quality. There are fewer mistakes and therefore less chances for the forwards. The level of concentration has to be so much higher.

"Playing alongside my 'minder' John Fashanu has been brilliant. When he's on song there is no better target man in the game. He is awesome and we seem to compliment each other on the pitch."

However, it has not all been plain sailing for Holdsworth, who suffered a severe knee injury when he was 17 that kept him out for over a year.

He struggled to make the grade with his first club Watford and while there had loan spells with four other clubs - Port Vale, Carlisle, Swansea and Brentford.

But while then Watford boss Steve Harrison was prepared to let him go, former Brentford manager Steve Perryman spotted a natural goalscorer and signed him for £150,000 in September 1989.

His career took off at Griffin Park, especially under Phil Holder, who succeeded Perryman as manager. In three seasons Holdsworth scored 75 goals in 137 games.

"Phil (Holder) was a great motivator and, with my youth coach at Watford, Tom Whalley, was the biggest influence on my career."

That career now seems to have no limits. If Holdsworth can maintain his prolific scoring rate, it surely will not be long before he is leading the England attack.

GARY MACKAY

HEARTS

MARK WALTERS
LIVERPOOL

WORLD

fact ● Paul Breitner scored the first goal of the 1974 World Cup tournament, for West Germany in a 1-0 win against Chile, and scored the last goal of the 1982 event, in a 3-1 defeat by Italy.

fact ● Only three of the 14 winners of World Cup tournaments won every match - Uruguay in 1930, Italy in 1938 (only four matches each) and Brazil in 1970 (six).

fact ● West Germany used 18 players in their six matches when winning the1954 tournament, and only two of them - Fritz Walter and Horst Eckel - played in all six. Brazil used only six players when winning in 1962, with ten of them ever-present.

fact ● Since the first World Cup in 1930 no fewer than 152 countries have competed for it, many of them failing to get through the qualifying stages. But only six nations have won it - Brazil ,Italy and Germany three times, Uruguay and Argentina twice, and England once.

Vava scores Brazil's first goal in their 1958 World Cup Final win over Sweden

fact. ● Brazil are the only nation to have taken part in all 14 tournaments. They have played a record 66 matches - not one of them at home - winning a record 44, drawing 11 , losing 11 and scoring a record 148 goals. West Germany have played 62, won 36, drawn 14, lost 12, and scored 131 goals.

fact. ● Bulgaria have the worst record of any nation to have made double-figure apperances in the final stages. They have played 16 games, drawn six and lost 10.

fact. ● Sixty players have been sent off in the final stages of the 14 World Cups - 21 in the first seven, 39 in the second seven. These include seven Argentinians, seven Brazilians and six Uruguayans.

CUP

facts

fact. ● The 14 finals have produced a total of 62 goals, 43 by winners and 19 by losers. Every team in those 14 matches scored at least once until Argentina lost 1-0 in 1990. Six teams lost after scoring twice: the last two occasions (1966 and 1986) both involved West Germany.

CONTINUED OVER

WORLDCUP *facts*

Mario Kempes scores against Holland in the 1978 Final

fact ● Alex Villaplane, captain of France in the 1930 World Cup, was executed by fellow-countrymen during World War Two, for collaborating with the occupying Germans.

fact ● Guilermo Stabile, top scorer in the 1930 World Cup with eight goals in four games for Argentina, only got into the team because the usual first choice dropped out in order to take a university exam.

fact ● In seven of the first ten finals, the nation scoring the first goal went on to LOSE. In contrast, the last four have been won by the team scoring first.

fact ● Only one manager or coach has taken the same country to the final stages of four World Cups: Walter Winterbottom of England in 1950-54-58-62.

fact ● The World Cup was in its sixth tournament before the first 0-0 draw in the final stages. That was between England and Brazil in 1958.

fact ● Jean Langenus of Belgium, who refereed the 1930 World Cup Final, combined that job with working as a journalist for German magazine.

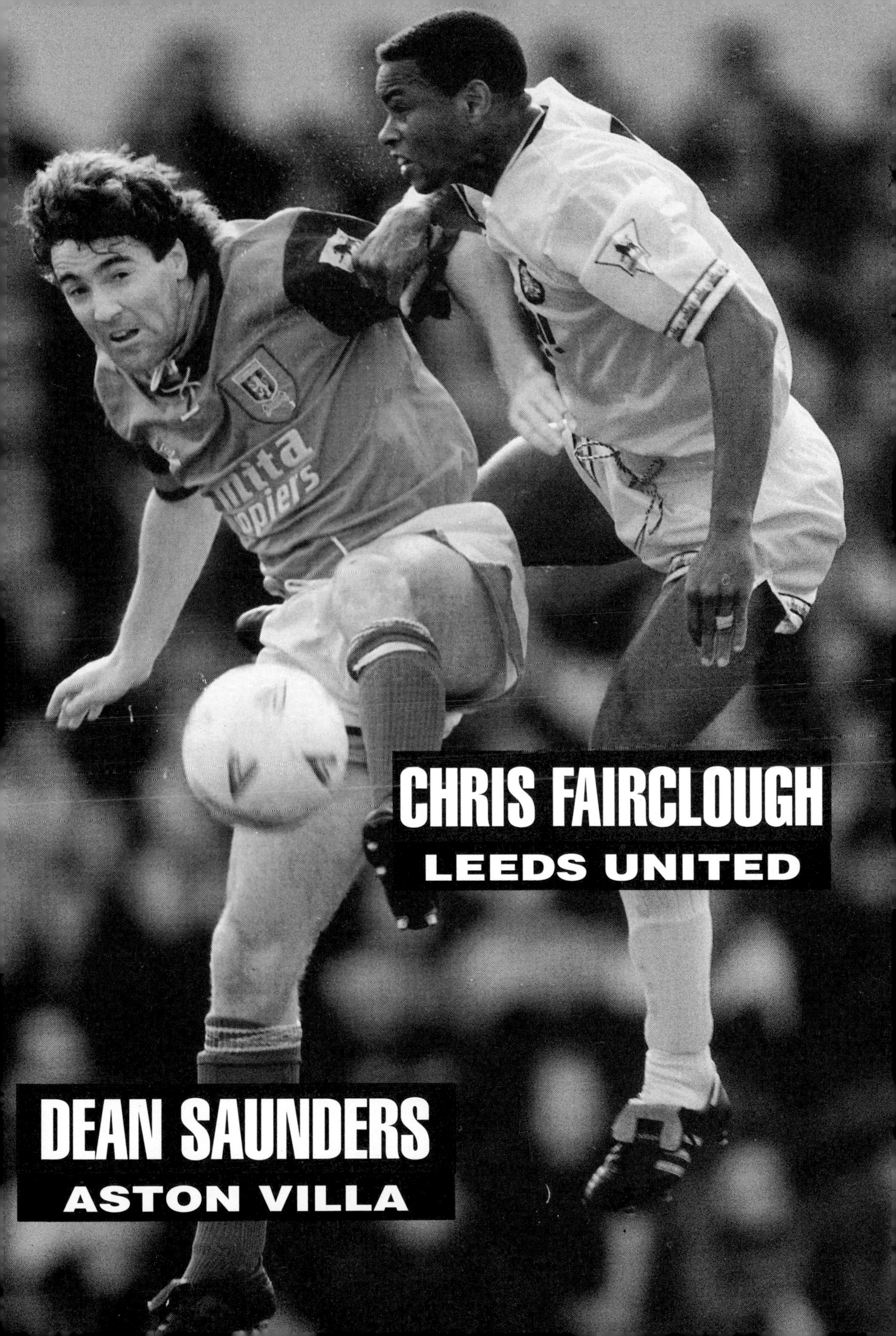

CHRIS FAIRCLOUGH
LEEDS UNITED

DEAN SAUNDERS
ASTON VILLA

Transfer Trail-Blazers!

MONEY makes the world go around, according to a well-known song. It also makes the ball go around if you pay enough of it.

Not long ago AC Milan were talking about paying £15 million for Ryan Giggs, Manchester United's Welsh wizard.

That's a long way away from that momentous day in 1905 when Britain witnessed its first four-figure transfer deal.

Striker Alf Common was a star in his own time. He played for England after starting his career with Sheffield United. He featured in the 1902 FA Cup Final which The Blades won against Southampton.

Later, Alf (above) was transferred to Sunderland. He also had a spell with Arsenal and was well-known to have a Gazza-type sense of humour and was the chief culprit of practical jokes in the dressing-room.

He really hit the headlines when Sunderland sold him to Middlesbrough for that sensational £1,000 in February 1905. The newspapers were full of transfer talk and there was even an enquiry by a special commission to ensure that nothing illegal had taken place.

Meanwhile Alf got on with doing what he did best — playing football. Desperate Middlesbrough were on the verge of relegation from the First Division and had not won away for two years.

Alf soon changed that, scoring from the penalty-spot to give his side a 1-0 success against his old club Sheffield United at Bramall Lane. Needless to say, Boro avoided the drop.

That was a milestone in the transfer trail. Today's milestones are in the millions with players like Alan Shearer busting the British bank at more than £3 million and the continental clubs happy to pay out four times that for the top men.

There have been some strange transfers along the way and some real bargains, too.

The newspapers went almost purple with excitement when Manchester United smashed all records in bringing Denis Law home from Torino in July 1962. United paid an amazing

£115,000 — an enormous amount of money to spend on a footballer at the time.

Newspaper headlines scream whenever there is a major transfer and the talk in the pubs, schools and grounds is of little else.

It was no different in 1928 when Alf Common's transfer fee became chicken feed. Arsenal took the plunge in buying superstar David Jack (above).

David had been the scorer of Bolton's first goal in that incredible FA Cup Final of 1923, the first at Wembley. He was also a regular England international and was without doubt one of the best players of that or any other day. No wonder Arsenal were prepared to pay big money for him — £10,890!

Today we see clubs buying young players for what might seem to be a fairly low fee which is then added to after the player has made a set number of appearances or been sold on for a profit. That's not really new.

When Arsenal signed Charlie Buchan (below) from Sunderland in 1925 they agreed a fee of £2,000 plus £100 for every goal he scored during his first season. He actually scored 19 times during that fee period.

Sometimes those extra clauses can get a bit complicated.

When Peter Watson left Irish club Newry Town for Aston Villa the initial fee was £800. But added to that were enough strings to make a decent goal net — £500 extra for 10 first team games; £500 extra for 20 reserve team games; £250 extra for a youth cap; £250 extra for an under-23 cap; £250 extra for a B international cap and £1,000 extra for a full cap. In the end Villa paid very little extra cash.

Sometimes clubs actually get a refund. In 1966 Huddersfield had to refund £18,000 of a £30,000 fee they received from Blackburn for Alan Gilliver after discovering a disc problem.

Blackburn sold Bill Campbell to Newton Heath (today's Manchester United) in 1894, but the Manchester club refused to pay the fee when it was discovered that Campbell suffered from rheumatism. The fee? £25.

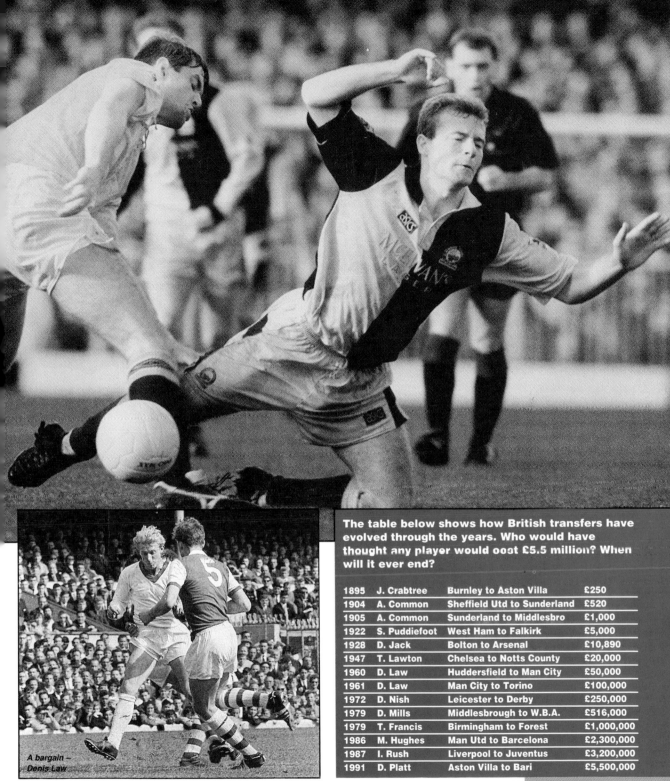

A bargain – Denis Law

The table below shows how British transfers have evolved through the years. Who would have thought any player would cost £5.5 million? When will it ever end?

Year	Player	Transfer	Fee
1895	J. Crabtree	Burnley to Aston Villa	£250
1904	A. Common	Sheffield Utd to Sunderland	£520
1905	A. Common	Sunderland to Middlesbro	£1,000
1922	S. Puddiefoot	West Ham to Falkirk	£5,000
1928	D. Jack	Bolton to Arsenal	£10,890
1947	T. Lawton	Chelsea to Notts County	£20,000
1960	D. Law	Huddersfield to Man City	£50,000
1961	D. Law	Man City to Torino	£100,000
1972	D. Nish	Leicester to Derby	£250,000
1979	D. Mills	Middlesbrough to W.B.A.	£516,000
1979	T. Francis	Birmingham to Forest	£1,000,000
1986	M. Hughes	Man Utd to Barcelona	£2,300,000
1987	I. Rush	Liverpool to Juventus	£3,200,000
1991	D. Platt	Aston Villa to Bari	£5,500,000

The transfer system was first put into operation in 1890 and it was based on the same system then in operation in the United States where baseball pioneered the transfer trail. In January 1908 the FA decided that enough was enough and put a maximum £350 limit on transfer deals. The arrangement lasted exactly four months.

One of the oddest transfers must have been on February 7th 1925 when Orient striker Albert Pape travelled with his side to play against Manchester United at Old Trafford. With kick-off just two hours away he was suddenly sold to United and actually played against Orient scoring in a 4-2 victory over his old club.

Of course, money does not always change hands — sometimes a free transfer is involved or even an exchange of players and then there are some really weird deals.

When Italian midfielder Guiseppe Murgia was transferred from Polisportira to Seulese the fee was a goat and a slice of ham and Republic of Ireland striker Tony Cascarino joined Gillingham for a some corrugated iron!

Contracts are signed in some funny places too — restaurants and hotels are quite normal — signings in cars on motorway service areas are not so uncommon, but there has only been one Commons signing — when Ian Lawther signed for Brentford from Scunthorpe in 1964 he actually signed in the House of Commons because The Bees chairman was Jack Dunnett MP.

GARY LINEKER

GRAMPUS EIGHT

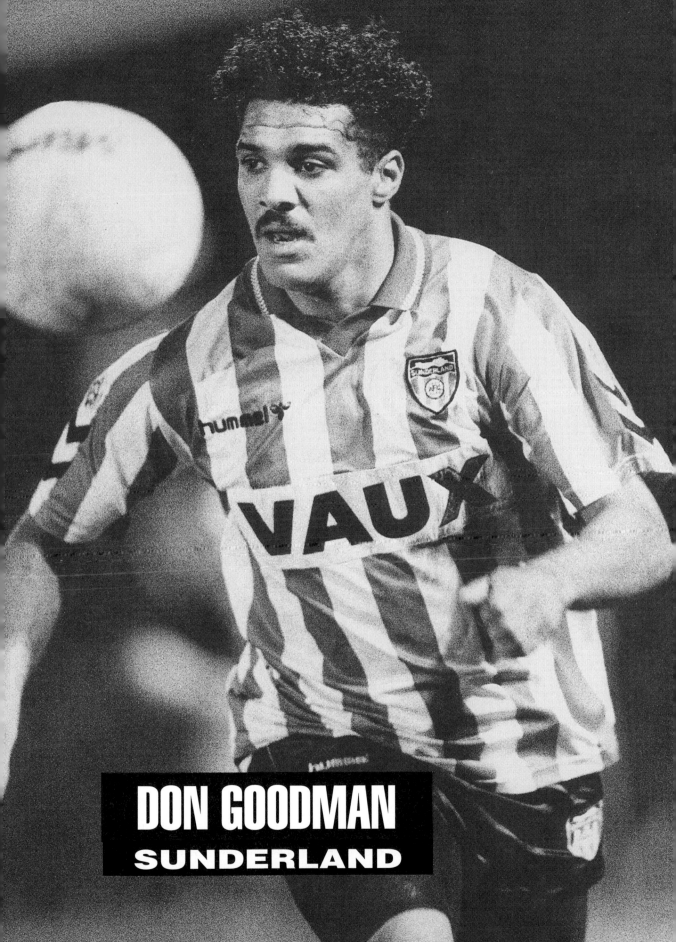

DON GOODMAN

SUNDERLAND

Football thrives in the
LAND OF THE

SOCCER in Japan was a totally unknown quantity in Britain until Gary Lineker decided to join Nagoya Grampus Eight in the newly-formed J League.

That led to wide publicity for Lineker, his club, and the Japanese game, with Fleet Street's finest duly turning up to watch until the novelty wore off.

But even though the Japanese have been cornering the media market over the past year or so, this is not the only country in the Far East where soccer is making strides. There's Hong Kong, as well.

Hong Kong is a British dependency, at least until the lease runs out and the nation reverts to Chinese rule. It is one of the most densely-populated places on earth, with a population of almost six million crammed into an area of little more than 1,000 square kilometres.

Not surprisingly, land is at a premium, but still football thrives amid the ranks of skyscrapers that stand like giant guardsmen everywhere you look.

There are 85 clubs registered with the Hong Kong FA (headquarters in quaintly-named Fat Kwong Street). There are nearly 4,000 registered players, including around 300 professionals. And for enthusiasm they're hard to beat,

Former Manchester United winger Ralph Milne (above) joined Sing Tao. Much travelled Iain Hesford (left) kept goal for Hull City.

even if it's hard to visualise their emergence as a world power.

THe HKFA are now nearly 70 years old, although a proper league did not come about until after World War Two. Early winners included Royal Air Force and Kowloon Motor Bus Company, but matters are now run on a genuinely competitive basis, and British visitors who pause amid their raids on the duty-free shops can be pleasantly surprised at the standard of play.

South China, the leading club, were formed in 1935 and took Arsenal's colours, red with white sleeves, in tribute to the London

club, who dominated English football around that period. In turn South China have dominated in HK, winning the championship 23 times.

Tradition

They are sponsored by Coca-Cola and have a tradition for finding young talent, reinforced by some importations with British experience. Brian McDermott (once with Arsenal), Allen McKnight (West Ham) and Steve Neville (Exeter) have been among them.

Dale Tempest (Huddersfield and Fulham) and much-travelled keeper Iain Hesford have reinforced the Eastern club in recent years, and another "wandering"

GIANTS

Allen McKnight (above), once a keeper with West Ham. Tony Sealey (right) now one of Hong Kong's finest imports.

keeper, Peter Guthrie, joined one-time Manchester United winger Ralph Milne at Sing Tao.

The most "decorated" Hong Kong import was Tony Sealy, who went to Michelotti soon after helping Brentford to the Third Division championship in 1991-92.

That was his FIFTH stint with a title-winning club during his career in England, following Crystal Palace (1979), QPR (83), Bournemouth (87), and Bristol Rovers (90).

He's the sort of lucky mascot Hong Kong soccer needs if it is to match the Lineker-inspired Japanese status in the Asian game.

super six bargain buys

They say that money makes the world go round but, even in these days of inflated transfers, there are still a few bargains around. And you won't find better value for money than this super six...

super six
MICK QUINN — Coventry

'He's fat, he's round, he's worth a million pound'. That's the chant that rings around Highfield Road these days when Mick Quinn takes the field.

At 31, he may not fetch £1 million, but he was certainly worth the £250,000 Bobby Gould forked out to take him from Newcastle.

Quinn has always maintained that he could score at any level and he proved it by hitting the target consistently in the Premier League.

The likeable Scouser, probably the slowest striker around, reckons he can beat anyone over a yard and 'after that, it's too late because the ball is in the back of the net'. There aren't too many defenders who'll argue.

What a barg

super six
MARK ROBSON — West Ham

Snapped up on a free transfer from Spurs, Robson quickly became a firm favourite with the Upton Park crowd. The West Ham fans have been brought up on skilful attackers and they love Robson's wizardry and trickery down the left flank.

He supplied the bullets for Clive Allen and Trevor Morley and also weighed in with a few vital goals of his own as West Ham regained their place in the top flight.

And Hammers' fans can rest easy about Robson's future. Manager Billy Bonds rewarded him with a new two-year contract towards the end of last season.

super six
DUNCAN SHEARER — Aberdeen

Shearer has scored goals wherever he's played and he had no trouble adapting to the Scottish Premier Division.

Some players find the difference between styles north and south of the border too much to cope with, but Shearer took it in his stride.

At £450,000 from Blackburn he was a steal, and Kenny Dalglish's loss was certainly Aberdeen's gain.

Manager Willie Miller will look to Shearer to bring out the best in Eoin Jess and Scott Booth as Aberdeen aim to end Rangers' dominance of the Premier League this season.

super six
CHRIS WADDLE — Sheffield Wednesday

OK, so he cost a £1 million. But when you consider some of the silly money spent on very average players, Waddle was cheap at three times the price.

And that was proved when Wednesday boss Trevor Francis turned down a £3 million pound offer from Nantes midway through last season.

Francis knew exactly what he was getting when he bought Waddle back to England from Marseille, and he wasn't disappointed.

The Geordie genius was simply outstanding as Wednesday enjoyed their best season for years.

When he's on song there's no better player in the country and it's a crying shame that his talent hasn't been rewarded with more England caps.

super six
NEIL RUDDOCK — Spurs

They say you should never go back to your old club but Ruddock disproved that theory.

He left Spurs six years ago after playing just 11 games but, after spells at Millwall and Southampton, he returned to White Hart Lane for £750,000.

And 'Razor' did as much as anyone to end, once and for all, Spurs' reputation as a soft touch.

The towering defender was an inspiration and also managed to shake off his 'bad boy' tag without losing any of his aggression.

He's been widely tipped for international honours and you can be sure Graham Taylor will be watching him.

super six
KEN MONKOU — Southampton

Monkou was an absolute revelation when he moved to The Dell from Chelsea.

At the time, the £750,000 fee looked to be a bit steep but the elegant defender would fetch at least twice that now.

His classy displays in the centre of The Saints' back four earned rave reviews and brought him to the attention of Holland boss Dick Advocaat.

If he continues in similar form this season, Southampton's biggest problem could be holding onto him when the big boys come sniffing.

What's

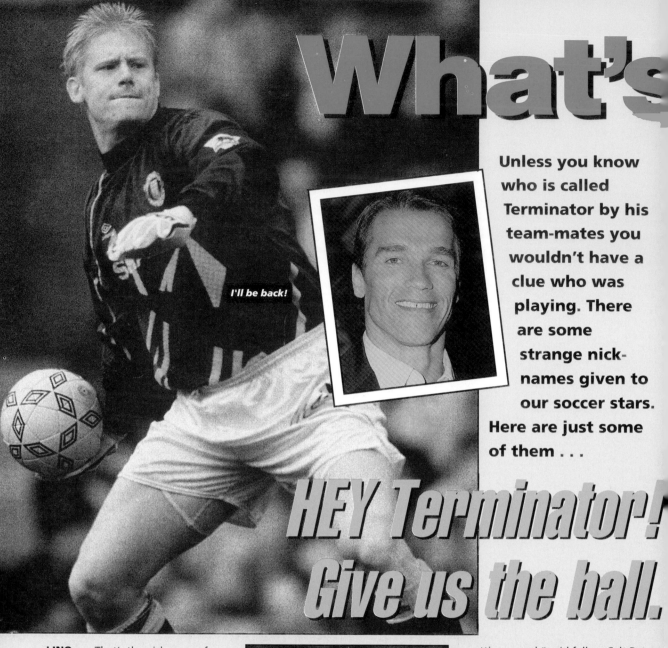

I'll be back!

Unless you know who is called Terminator by his team-mates you wouldn't have a clue who was playing. There are some strange nick-names given to our soccer stars. Here are just some of them . . .

HEY Terminator! Give us the ball.

LINO . . . That's the nickname of Ipswich goal ace Chris Kiwomya. He was given the name by former team manager John Lyall.

"He gave me the name Lino, short for linoleum, because he said I spent so much time on the ground," Chris explained. "I was just trying to make an impression with some acrobatic stuff and I kept ending up on the deck."

TRIGGER . . . One of the most popular characters in BBC TV's hilarious Only Fools and Horses. We know of at least two players with that nickname. One is Liverpool's Rob Jones (right) — "We call him that because he's a bit slow on the uptake," said team-mate Ian Rush.

Another is Gerry Creaney of Celtic. "It's because he looks like him when he smiles after

getting a goal," said fellow Celt Peter Grant.

Over at Rangers Mark Hateley has come in for some stick because of his hair-style. His Ibrox mates have taken to calling him **CHIPPENDALE**. At least we hope that's the reason! Richard Gough was named **STORMIN' NORMAN** when he had close cropped hair like the American military general. But spare a thought for goalkeeper Andy Goram. He was nicknamed **BARNEY RUBBLE** because his team-mates believe he looks like the cartoon character from the Flintstones.

Hair seems to play a great part in picking nicknames for players, just ask Liverpool's David Burrows who was tagged **BART SIMPSON** because of his. But it's not only hair — ears can earn you a special title too.

in a name?

Justin Edinburgh is known as **PRINCE CHARLES** because of his outstanding lugs while team-mate Steve Sedgley is called **ET** because he has a long neck. Our favourite is Darren Anderton being called **SICKNOTE** during his Portsmouth days because he always claimed to have something wrong with him.

On the other side of London, Queens Park Rangers star Andy Sinton revealed the nicknames of a couple of his mates. "Dennis Bailey (right) is called **BILLY GRAHAM** (inset) because of his religious interests and Ian Holloway is publicly called **HOLLY**. There are other nicknames I can't tell you about but it is to do with the fact that we reckon he is hyperactive and has four children."

Not all nicknames are for taking the mickey. Manchester United's Brian

McClair is called **CHOCCY** after the the well known cake (chocolate McClair - geddit!). Less original is the fact that Peter Schmeichel has been dubbed **THE TERMINATOR** because the United lads believe he has the looks of Arnold Schwarzenegger's famous character.

Blackburn's Jason Wilcox is often called **ARNIE** because he enjoys weight training and at Norwich they have given Ian Butterworth the nickname **SPARTACUS** because he is a fitness fanatic.

Not everyone gets a nickname, though. Tony Cottee admitted that at Everton they have no pet name for goalkeeper Neville Southall. "We wouldn't dare give him a nickname — we're all scared of him," said Cottee. No doubt you have your own nicknames for your favourite players but here are a few more to remember:

MORE NICKNAMES

PAUL ALLEN (SPURS) — SQUEAKY. It's because of his voice.

RONNIE ROSENTHAL (LIVERPOOL) — The Shekel. He's Israeli.

MICHAEL THOMAS (LIVERPOOL) — MICKEY THE HAT. He buys and wears lots of different hats.

STEVE MCMANAMAN (LIVERPOOL) —SHAGGY. The others say he always looks scruffy even when he is wearing new clothes so they named him after the cartoon character in "Scooby Doo".

DAVID RUSH (SUNDERLAND) — BUNGALOW. His mates say it is because he hasn't a lot upstairs. Once when the opposing team held up a No. 7 to make their substitution, he trotted off the pitch.

MARK BOWEN (NORWICH) and **IAN FERGUSON (RANGERS)** are both called **ALBERT TATLOCK.** Their team-mates say they moan a lot, just like the former Coronation Street character.

STUART MCCALL (RANGERS) — OLIVER REED. It's because he likes lager.

OLEG KUZNETSOV (RANGERS) — OLLIE OR SHIRLEY. Ollie is obvious but Ian Durrant calls him Shirley

because of his curly blond hair.

ANTON ROGAN (CELTIC) — ALGIPAN. He gets hot and goes red easily.

MARK HUGHES (MANCHESTER UNITED) — SPARKY. Ron Atkinson gave him the name as a compliment.

KEITH HILL (BLACKBURN) — GIPPO. They say he looks like a gypsy.

LEE RICHARDSON (BLACKBURN) — THE TRAMP. Another who has expensive clothes but still looks scruffy.

NIGEL CLOUGH (NOTTINGHAM FOREST) — CLOG. That's how Staurt Pearce believes his name should be pronounced.

MARK CROSSLEY (NOTTINGHAM FOREST) — NORMAN. They say he looks like Norman Whiteside.

STUART PEARCE (NOTTINGHAM FOREST) — PSYCHO. Needs no explanation. The original.

TONY ADAMS (ARSENAL) — RODDERS. Team-mates think he looks like Rodney Trotter from Only Fools and Horses.

BOBBY MIMMS (BLACKBURN) — JOE MANGLE. They say he looks like the character from Neighbours.

CRAIG LEVEIN (HEARTS) — SHOES. The Hearts gang think he looks like Neil from The Young Ones so they named him Shoes.

JIM BETT (ABERDEEN) — JAZZER. Has been called that for years — even his wife uses that name for him.

TONY COTON (MANCHESTER CITY) — COLONEL MUSTARD. He once wore a bright yellow jacket.

GRAEME LE SAUX (BLACKBURN) — BERGE. He comes from Jersey — like Bergerac.

DENNIS WISE (CHELSEA) — THE RAT. He's always up to no good with practical jokes.

CARLTON PALMER (SHEFFIELD WEDNESDAY) — LIGHTBULB HEAD OR SWIMCAP HEAD. You ask him!

ALAN HARPER (EVERTON) — BERTIE. He plays in "all sorts" of positions.

CHRIS WHYTE (LEEDS) — HUGGY BEAR. After the character in Starsky and Hutch.

DAVID BATTY (LEEDS) — ANIMAL. It's because he enjoys five-a-sides in training.

YOU WON'T BELIEVE IT but it's true!

A look at the amazing world of soccer

Fishy tale

● ONE of the most unusual fan clubs must be the Manchester branch of the Queen of the South supporters. There are 30 of them who meet regularly and go to matches together. None of them have any Scottish connection other than supporting the team which came about because they like the name. They have a special initiation ceremony for new members as founder John Igoe explained.

"New members have to swear undying loyalty to Queens while holding a frozen trout under their right arm and a 'Joe 90' Annual in their left hand. They then have to drink a tin of cold scotch broth before they're signed on." There's no answer to that really is there?

Crazy ritual

●NEW arrivals at our soccer clubs are often the butt of practical jokes and crazy ceremonies, but nothing beats the ritual that England star Les Ferdinand went through when he joined Turkish club Besiktas. In a very serious ceremony he was daubed with sheep's blood! Certainly beats being thrown in the bath with your clothes on.

Match that!

● HOW do you get to play 48 League matches in a season? Simply by changing clubs. Scottish international Tommy Walker did it during the 1946-47 season. He started the season early with Hearts and was then transferred to Chelsea. By the end of the season he had chalked up that record 48 league matches in one season.

Driving force

● EVER since Chris Waddle admitted that he used to be a sausage maker there has been a lot of interest in the jobs players might have done if they hadn't made it to soccer stardom. Stuart Pearce is just one of several who are qualified electricians, Manchester United's Steve Bruce came as close as you could get to becoming a plumber, an offer coming to join Gillingham only a day or two before he was due to start a new job. But perhaps one of the most apt is the idea of John Wark. The Ipswich and Scotland star would have become a driving instructor. Well, he is certainly a driving force when he's playing and even referees have received instructions from him.

On and off!

● HOW about this for a quick red card. Bologna striker Guiseppe Lorenzo was sent on as substitute in the match against Parma in the 72nd minute. A corner was about to be taken and was held up while the substitution was made. What happened next? The referee was about to blow the whistle for the corner to be taken when he suddenly saw the linesman waving his flag like mad. He went over and spoke to him and immediately sent off Lorenzo for striking an opponent. Lorenzo had been on the pitch for no more than 10 seconds!

Neighbours?

● SUNDERLAND fan Sandra Hall wanted to live near her hero Marco Gabbiadini so when she noticed a house for sale just a few doors away she convinced her husband that it would be a good idea to move. Husband Alan actually agreed and the day of the big move was set. Only problem was that just a couple of days before, Sunderland sold Marco to Crystal Palace so Sandra had to be content with sending him a good luck message and telling her friends that she now lives near where Marco Gabbiadini used to live.

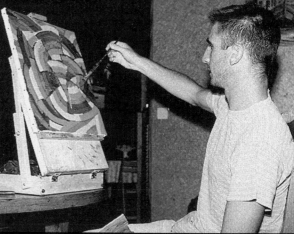

Rambo

● WHEN a soccer newshound tried to get a scoop interview with famous Frenchman Monsieur Eric Cantona, he asked the supershrugger who his hero was. Eric, a lover of art and other fine things immediately said "Rimbaud". The reporter, who thought art was one half of Simon and Garfunkel, wrote down Rambo and as a result the bemused Cantona began to receive pictures of Sylvester Stallone from his many fans. Needless to say the reporter is now back to doing write-ups on jumble sales.

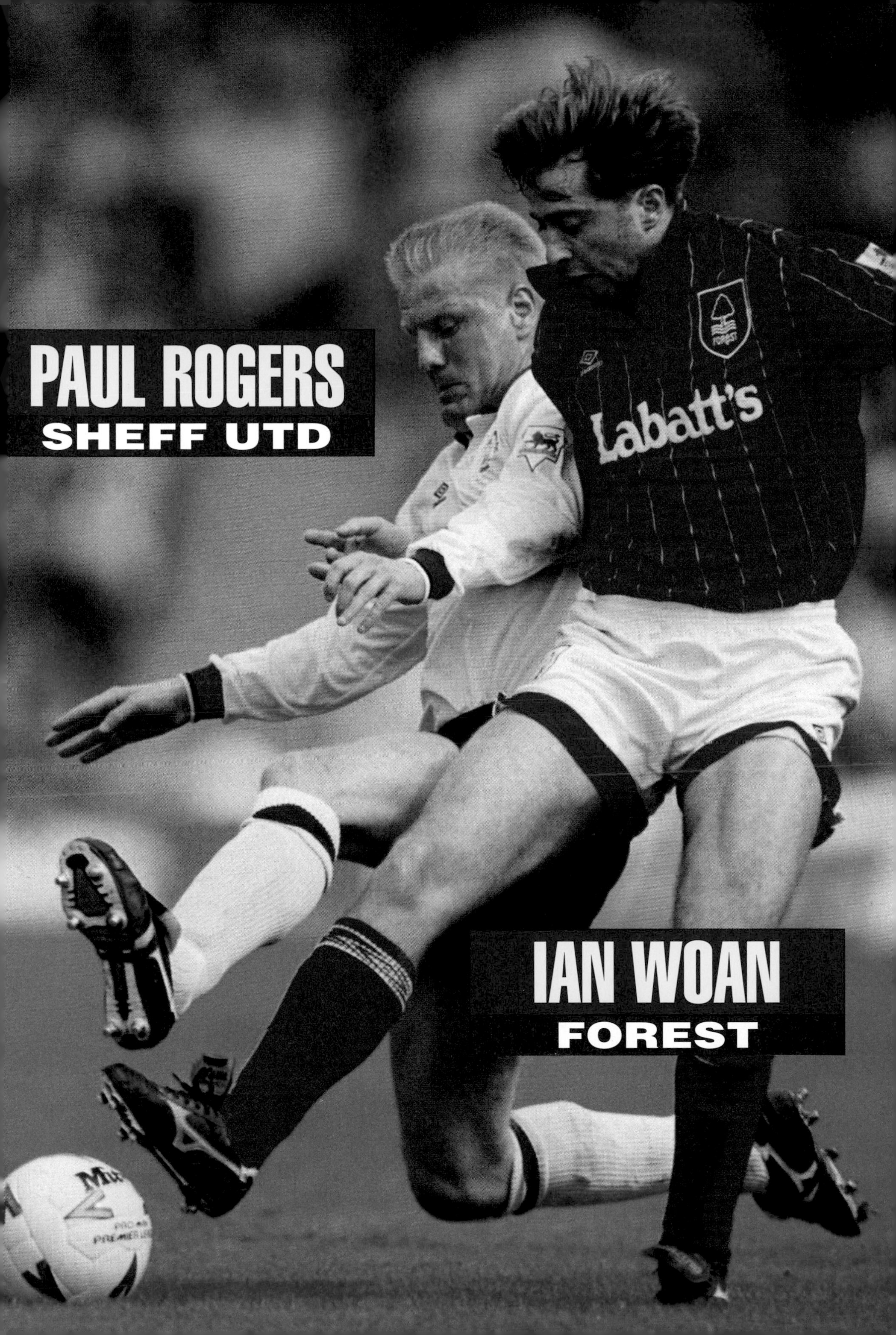

PAUL ROGERS
SHEFF UTD

IAN WOAN
FOREST

WAS MY

Players recall the

WE'VE all done it, haven't we? We've all had that moment when we would like the ground to open and swallow us up to hide us from our embarrassment.

Leeds and England star **DAVID BATTY** recalls the moment that made his face red when the ground really did seem to open up.

"I was walking home one night after an evening out. Suddenly my leg went through a hole in the pavement. It was actually one of those basement skylights and it had broken.

"I wasn't hurt, but my leg stuck fast and the fire brigade had to come and rescue me. My face was redder than their fire engine," David recalls.

Some of the Manchester United stars admit to having had faces redder than their shirts. Skipper **STEVE BRUCE** still laughs about his unforgettable face-flushing moment.

"I was demonstrating ball control to a group of schoolkids. I was showing off a little bit and they were looking on suitably impressed. Then I tripped over the ball. They laughed and I went red — very red."

Steve also helped a team-mate recount his worst moment. **PAUL INCE** believes his most embarrassing moment was when he was travelling with Steve Bruce.

They were in Steve's car and ran out of petrol. Paul had to push the car to the nearest

petrol station, much to the delight of the many passers-by, who thought it was enormously funny to see the two United superstars in such a fix.

Old Trafford team-mate Lee Martin chuckled over his red-faced moment.

"We were having a quiet meal out at a local restaurant and keeping a low profile," said Lee. "It was all going well until I fell down the stairs. There was silence for a moment then a lot of loud laughter at my expense. I don't think I've had the nerve to show my face there since".

Sheffield Wednesday star **CHRIS WADDLE** recalls this magic moment from his time in France, with mighty Marseille.

"I don't get embarrassed easily, but I certainly reddened this time," said Chris. "I was sitting in a restaurant and poured myself a glass of golden coloured wine from a small carafe. When I sipped it I found I was drinking olive oil! It was hysterical — to everyone else!"

Worse things can happen of course

— as **TONY DORIGO**, Leeds and England star, found out during what was supposed to have been a celebration. He was playing for Chelsea at the time.

"It was my 23rd birthday and we decided to have a good party. It was going fine until a kiss-o-gram arrived, organised by my wife, Heather. The kiss-o-gram girl weighed 20 stone!

"It took me a long time to live that down and there are still some photos around, though I'd rather not see them!"

It's not always off the pitch that those best-forgotten times occur. Own goals can be very embarrassing. Arsenal and England 'keeper **DAVID SEAMAN** didn't exactly score an own goal, but he did the next best thing.

FACE RED
most embarrassing moments ...

"I was playing for Peterborough at the time. We were up against York. I took the ball and threw it out straight away to launch an attack. Unfortunately, I launched an attack for York as I threw the ball straight to one of their forwards who said thank you very much and planted it in the net. That took some living down I can tell you!"

Coventry's American international **ROY WEGERLE** did score an own goal, but he did it in style. He lobbed the ball past his own goalkeeper in front of 40,000 Arsenal fans at Highbury. There was nowhere for Roy to hide as The Gunners fans cheerfully called his name.

Back to the goalkeepers and the great **PETER SHILTON** readily admits that even he has had moments he would rather pretend never happened.

"I was playing for Stoke against Newcastle and we were 1-0 up with only a minute to go. Alan Gowling, the Newcastle forward, chased a through ball, but he had no real chance of catching it. I calmly ran out to boot it up the field and completely missed it.

"I ended up in heap on the floor colliding with Alan but he was up in a flash and helped the ball into the net.

"It didn't end there though. I reported for England duty the next day and of course, all the lads had seen it on television. They really gave me some stick!"

DARREN ANDERTON of Spurs also recalls his most

embarrassing moment for us. It was on the pitch when he was playing for Portsmouth.

"I picked the ball up to take a quick throw-in and the referee pulled me up. I really complained and moaned about it but he was only stopping play to tell me it was a corner. I felt really silly after moaning so much."

Away from soccer England star **DAVID PLATT** has only one really bad moment to recall.

"I playfully jumped on the back of my brother — then I discovered it wasn't my brother. I didn't know what to say and that bloke whose back I had just jumped on thought I was a complete idiot. He was probably right!"

Wimbledon striker **DEAN HOLDSWORTH** believes his most reddening time came when he was playing cricket!

"I was playing for Watford at cricket when my trousers fell down. If that wasn't embarrassing enough, the commentator got on the mike and asked me if I needed a belt. That made sure that nobody in the ground missed what had happened."

But perhaps the very worst moment of all belongs to Oldham's **PAUL BERNARD**.

"It was during my apprenticeship at Oldham," he says. "I got forced into doing a party piece at the Christmas do. I had to sing a song while stark naked in front of the entire playing staff using a broom handle as a microphone. I'll never forget it — nobody will let me!"

WORLD CUP USA 94

THE 1994 World Cup Finals in the USA is only months away now and Europe are playing away. Once again the cream of soccer will be gathered to contest the greatest sports tournament on earth.

Some lucky SHOOT readers will be there, but for most of us we shall have to rely on television.

Here's a sneak preview of some of the top names in Europe we can expect to see taking on the rest of the world to keep the trophy on the continent where it has been for the last four years.

SWEDEN

Tomas Brolin:
Superstar of Swedish soccer. A national hero as a teenager, Brolin (below) has grown up while playing in Italy and now has maturity to add to his obvious skills.

Jan Eriksson:
Keeps the defence together, but also good on the break. He's capable of turning defence into attack with one swift move. Great feed for Brolin.

FRANCE

Jean-Pierre Papin:
Past European Footballer of the Year, Papin (above) is one of the most dangerous goalscorers around. Playing alongside so many stars in the Milan team might make him look ordinary, but watch out if he's about.

Eric Cantona:
Needs little introduction to English soccer fans. We all know he can make something out of nothing with just one flick of a foot. A lethal combination with Papin that could be a World Cup winner.

HOLLAND

Marco Van Basten:
If Holland are there they will not be without the world's top player. No half-measures with Marco (right), he is either out of touch or simply sensational. The world's top striker.

Dennis Bergkamp:
Another of Europe's top stars. A sharp attacker with the ability to create or score. The combination of himself with Van Basten on a day when they both hit top form would be just about unstaoppable.

EURO CRATS

BELGIUM

Enzo Scifo:
Belgium's megastar (above), he plays for Torino in Italy. Brilliant individual player, but also motivates the team.

Philippe Albert:
Young defender and definitely one to watch. Quite new to the national side, but has turned into a key man. Hard but fair, he is the king-pin of the Belgian rearguard.

DENMARK

Brian Laudrup:
Sensational forward (left) whose game has been sharpened by playing in Italy. Tricky and skilful, he'll cause problems for any defence.

Peter Schmeichel:
One of the world's top goalkeepers, he fills the goal with his size. He also fills his defence with confidence. And he has exceptional reactions for such a big man.

ITALY

Gianluigi Lentini:
The most expensive footballer in Europe when AC Milan paid £13 for him. On his day, he's a brilliant attacking midfielder and a real threat.

Franco Baresi:
Still at the top of his game, Baresi (left) is a player with vast experience. He already has a World Cup winners medal having been in the 1982 squad. The best defender in the world.

GERMANY

Thomas Hassler:
One of the best midfielders in Europe and very keen to earn another World Cup winners medal. The Roma star will take some stopping.

Jurgen Klinsmann:
Plays for Monaco after sampling life in Italy. Fast and furious attacker (above), he wants to quit the soccer high-life after the 1994 World Cup. Also in the winning side in 1990.

AND OTHERS:

Tomas Skuhravy (Czech)
One of the top strikers in Italy, where he plays for Genoa. Big and strong, he will be a handful for any defence if the Czechs make it to the finals in the USA.

Paolo Futre (Portugal)
Lethal attacker who now plays for Benfica, after a successful spell with Atletico Madrid. He's adored by his countrymen and is a sensational player.

Hristo Stoichkov (Bulgaria):
A gutsy attacker who gained that extra something while playing for Barcelona. Rated second only to Van Basten in Europe.

Rafael Martin-Vazquez (Spain):
If Spain make it all the way he could be the name on everyone's lips. Starred with Marseille before a £3.3 million move to Real Madrid. Attacking midfielder.

Rune Bratseth (Norway):
A national hero in Norway, but he plays in Germany and helped Werder Bremen to the 1992 European Cup-Winners' Cup. A dominant defender who is a real attacking threat.

Andrezej Juskoviak (Poland):
Top scorer in the 1992 Olympic Games and won a silver medal. Now he is in Poland's senior squad and has become a real attacking threat since signing for Sporting Lisbon.

WELSH

WHATEVER happens next to Wales, there is no doubt that they have made their mark in recent years on the world scene.

Victories over the likes of Brazil, Belgium and Germany have been nothing less than sensational.

Welsh football is ablaze with hope for the future and is probably stronger now than during its great days of the 1930s when the country were outright Home International Champions three times.

Terry Yorath has been manager of Wales since July 1988 and has masterminded the soccer fire in the land of the Red Dragon. But Terry will admit that his super spell would not be possible without his Welsh wizards who have put the magic back into football both on the hillsides and in the valleys of Wales.

Shoot pays tribute to the Boyos doing the business for Wales.

NEVILLE SOUTHALL

Ace goalkeeper and on his day one of the very best in the world. He is an awesome character for opposing attackers. Big Nev was born in Llandudno in September 1958 and began his career with Bury. He was soon snapped up by Everton and apart from a brief loan spell with Port Vale has been at Goodison non-stop for 12 seasons. Southall has around 70 caps to his credit and started in 1982 with a victory and clean-sheet against Northern Ireland.

IAN RUSH

The greatest international scorer in the history of Welsh football. His first full cap was against Scotland in 1980 and he has never looked back. He was born in St. Asaph in October 1961 and has spent most of his career with Liverpool after starting with Chester. Ian had a brief spell with Juventus, but was happy to return to Merseyside. A World Cup goal against Belgium in March took his tally to 24 - a new Welsh record.

MARK HUGHES

Sparky is still the livewire of the side. Apart from spells with Barcelona and Bayern Munich, Mark has been a Manchester United man all his playing life. Mark's full Welsh cap came in 1984 against England in an historic 1-0 win. Since then he has been a regular in the side with more than 50 caps to his credit. Mark was born in Wrexham in November 1963 and made his Welsh debut in his home town.

MARK BOWEN

One of the unsung heroes of Wales. Mark has more than 20 caps and has been in the squad since his full debut on tour against Canada in 1986. Now with Norwich, Mark was previously with Spurs but was born in Neath in December 1963. He is a hard-worker who players anywhere but prefers defence.

DAVE PHILLIPS

With more than 40 caps, Dave Phillips is another of the more experienced members of the Welsh squad. He was born in Wegberg in Germany in July 1963, but qualified through his parents to play for Wales. Dave made his debut for his country in that remarkable 1-0 win over England in 1984, the same day as Mark Hughes. Dave's career has spanned Plymouth, Manchester City, Coventry and Norwich.

BARRY HORNE

Another Everton star who has previously played for Wrexham, Portsmouth and Southampton. Equally at home in defence or midfield, Barry has 40 caps under his belt having started his international career in September 1987 when Denmark were beaten 1-0. Barry was born in May 1962 in the same place as Ian Rush - St. Asaph.

GARY SPEED

Compared with most of the others Gary is one of the new kids on the block. He was born in Hawarden in September 1969. His bread and butter soccer career has been solely at Leeds, but his international career has seen every stage of Welsh football from schools to senior. His first full cap was in 1990 when Wales beat Costa Rica 1-0. He now has more than 20 caps to his name and there will be many more in the future.

WIZARDS

ERIC YOUNG

Eric made his Welsh debut on the same day as Gary Speed in that victory over Costa Rica. He was actually born in Singapore in March 1960, but qualified to play for Wales under special international rules. A rocky defender, Eric played for Brighton, Wimbledon and then Crystal Palace before fully establishing his international credentials.

DEAN SAUNDERS

Another Welsh superstar who could one day overcome the Rush goal record. Saunders started his career with Swansea and was actually given a free transfer by them. Later he played for Cardiff, Brighton, Oxford and Derby before hitting the headlines with Liverpool and now, of course, with Aston Villa. Dean was born in Swansea in June 1964 and his international debut came in 1986 with a 1-0 win over Eire in Dublin.

RYAN GIGGS

Probably the most exciting player in Britain and perhaps even in Europe. Ryan was born in Cardiff in November 1973. He actually played for England as a schoolboy, but then went on to represent his native Wales at all other levels, making his first full appearance as a substitute in 1992 in a defeat at the hands of Germany. Another Manchester United star, Ryan is probably the ace in the Welsh pack and the hero of his country.

THERE are many others still waiting in the wings - Chris Coleman of Crystal Palace; Andy Melville of Oxford and Derby's Mark Pembridge are just some of the great examples of the new depth to Welsh soccer. There is an exciting crop of young players storming through the Under-21 squad as well.

These are still early days for the Welsh wizards, but there are some spellbinding moments ahead.

STAR TREK:

It was less than four years ago that Jack Charlton's Republic of Ireland shook the soccer world to its foundations with their battling displays at the 1990 World Cup finals.

Few people were prepared to take the men in green too seriously before those finals kicked off. Big Jack's laid-back approach and long-ball style convinced the experts that the Irish all-sorts were just going along for the ride. How wrong they were.

Italia 90 heralded the arrival of the Republic of Ireland as a major force in world soccer as they swept their way to the Quarter-Finals and gave host nation Italy the fright of their lives before bowing out with heads held high.

Now Jack's lads are all geared up for another World Cup assault at USA '94 and this time no-one will underestimate them. Many of the old faces have survived from Italia 90 to fight another World Cup campaign, but others won't be quite so familiar to the watching world. SHOOT salutes Ireland's new generation.

TERRY PHELAN

Position: Left-back
Debut: Sept 91 v Hungary
Caps to summer 93: 12
The most expensive defender in British football, the international arrival of the Manchester City full-back has allowed Charlton to move Steve Staunton into midfield. Strong in the tackle and blessed with exceptional pace, Phelan's deep runs and crosses are ideally suited for team-mate Niall Quinn.

ALAN KELLY

Position: Goalkeeper
Debut: Feb 93 v Wales
Caps to summer 93: 1
The Sheffield United 'keeper (above) has emerged as a realistic challenger to Pat Bonner and is now ready to take over as Eire's No.1. The son of former Republic of Ireland goalkeeper Alan Kelly, he was outstanding for The Blades last season and is set for another ten years at the top.

ALAN KERNAGHAN

Position: Centre-half
Debut: Sept 92 v Latvia
Caps to summer 93: 3
Like many of Charlton's team, the powerful Middlesbrough defender (right) was born in England but qualifies for the Republic through Irish grandparents. Played for Northern Ireland as a schoolboy but is now ready and waiting to take over from the veteran Kevin Moran for the Republic.

THE NEXT GENERATION

DENNIS IRWIN

Position: Right-back
Debut: Sept 90 v Morocco
Caps to summer 93: 18
Has hardly put a foot wrong since joining Manchester United in 1990 and was one of the unsung heroes of last season's Championship campaign. A left-back for United, Irwin (right) has proved his versatility with Eire by performing just as steadily on the right of their defence.

ROY KEANE

Position: Midfield
Debut: May 1991 v Chile
Caps to summer 93: 13
Just turned 22 and destined to become one of Ireland's all-time greats. It was less than three years ago that Nottingham Forest bought him from Irish part-timers Cobh Ramblers for just £10,000. Now he's worth close on £5 million and the sky is the limit. Already an established member of Charlton's midfield, he could be the sensation of USA '94.

EDDIE McGOLDRICK

Position: Utility man
Debut: March 92 v Switzerland
Caps to summer 93: 8
A relative latecomer to international football, McGoldrick (above) is an ideal squad member because of his versatility. Made his mark for Crystal Palace as a winger before switching to sweeper. The Republic have also used him as left-back in Phelan's absence, where his accurate passing and crossing are a great asset.

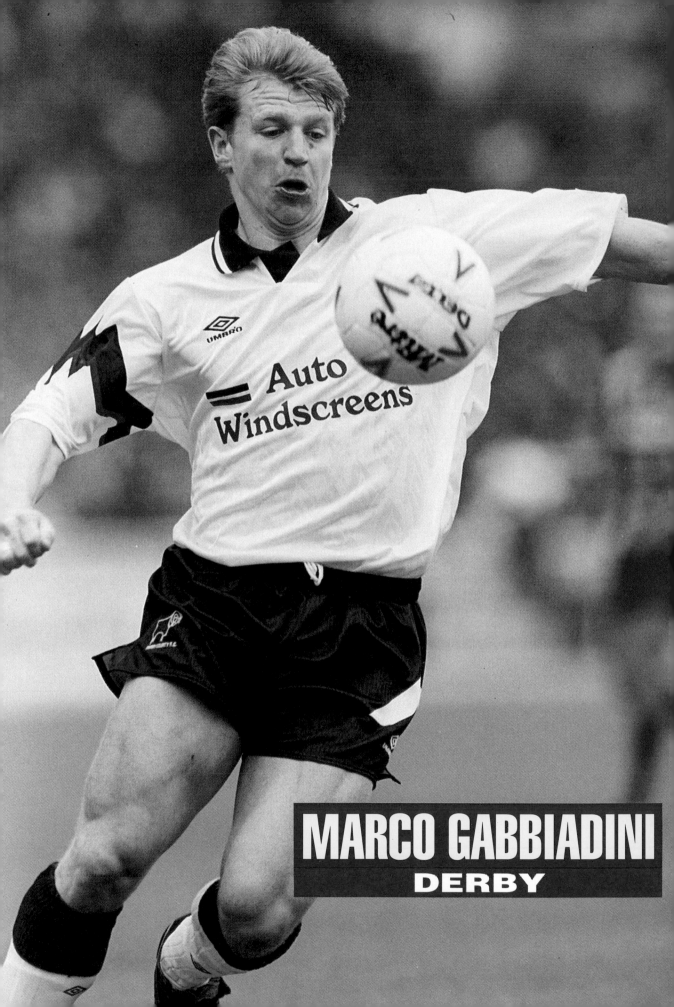

MARCO GABBIADINI
DERBY

DAVID LINIGHAN

IPSWICH

PRIZE

Paul McGrath's immaculate displays in the centre of Aston Villa's defence last season earned him the PFA Player of the Year award. The Republic of Ireland international has defied near crippling knee injuries to continue his career at the top level and, if anything, seems to be getting better with age. So heaven help the rest of the Premier League when he gets to 40!

GUYS

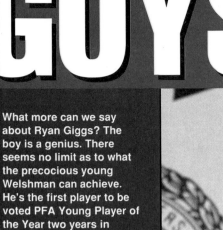

What more can we say about Ryan Giggs? The boy is a genius. There seems no limit as to what the precocious young Welshman can achieve. He's the first player to be voted PFA Young Player of the Year two years in succession and that, surely, is just the first of many records which will come Ryan's way in the next few years.

It's testimony to Andy Goram's outstanding ability that he was named Player of the Year in Scotland in the season that Rangers scored more goals than anyone else in Britain, with Ally McCoist weighing in with 50 of his own! But still Goram got the vote and that says everything about him. He's cool and unflappable and has now firmly established himself as his country's first choice 'keeper.

DENNIS WISE
CHELSEA

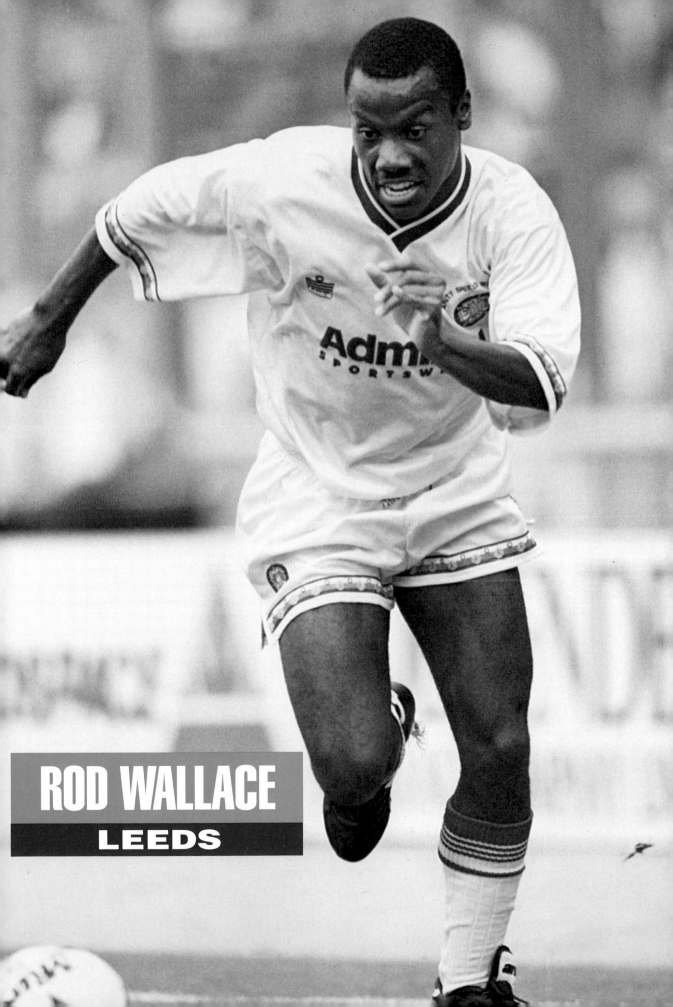

ROD WALLACE
LEEDS

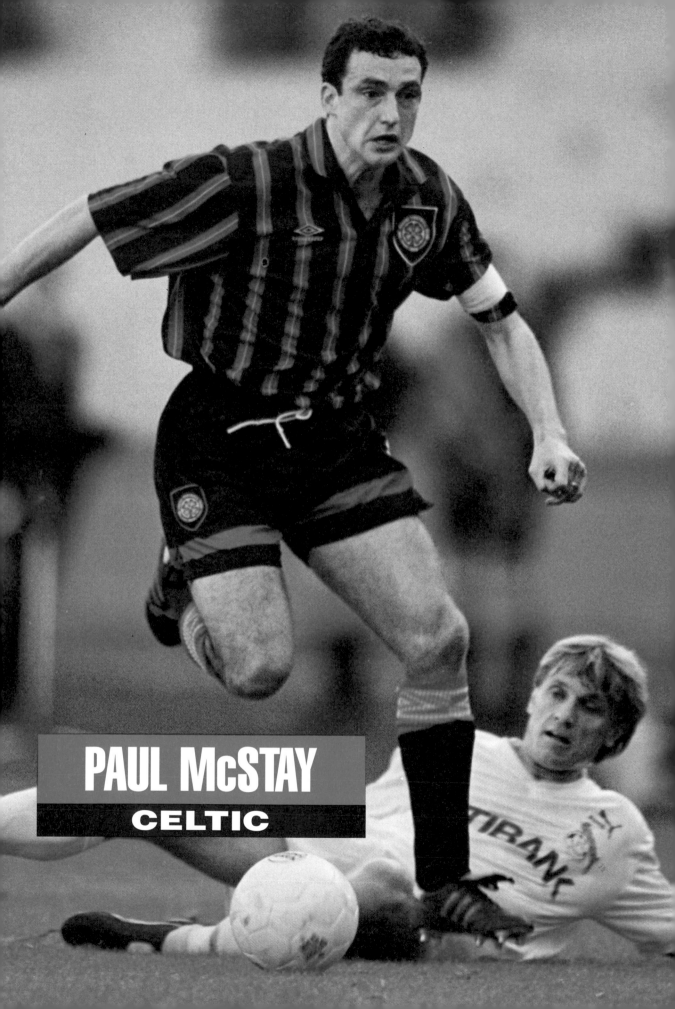

PAUL McSTAY

CELTIC

PAUL INCE
MAN UTD

GOALS, GOALS

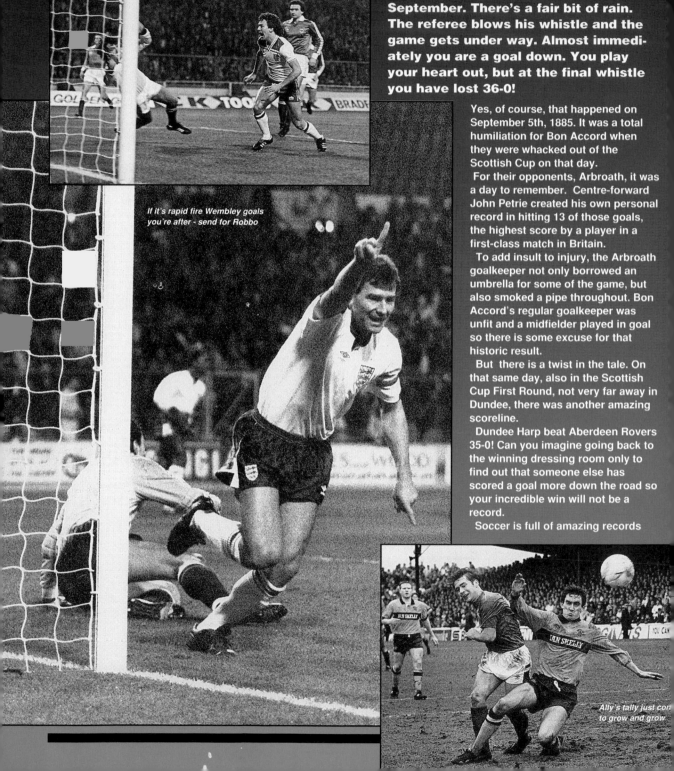

IMAGINE the scene. You are lined up for the kick-off in a First Round Cup-tie. The weather is not very good even for September. There's a fair bit of rain. The referee blows his whistle and the game gets under way. Almost immediately you are a goal down. You play your heart out, but at the final whistle you have lost 36-0!

Yes, of course, that happened on September 5th, 1885. It was a total humiliation for Bon Accord when they were whacked out of the Scottish Cup on that day.

For their opponents, Arbroath, it was a day to remember. Centre-forward John Petrie created his own personal record in hitting 13 of those goals, the highest score by a player in a first-class match in Britain.

To add insult to injury, the Arbroath goalkeeper not only borrowed an umbrella for some of the game, but also smoked a pipe throughout. Bon Accord's regular goalkeeper was unfit and a midfielder played in goal so there is some excuse for that historic result.

But there is a twist in the tale. On that same day, also in the Scottish Cup First Round, not very far away in Dundee, there was another amazing scoreline.

Dundee Harp beat Aberdeen Rovers 35-0! Can you imagine going back to the winning dressing room only to find out that someone else has scored a goal more down the road so your incredible win will not be a record.

Soccer is full of amazing records

If it's rapid fire Wembley goals you're after - send for Robbo

Ally's tally just con to grow and grow

GOALS GALORE!

and goalscoring seems to provide some of the best. Still in Scotland there is one record that is being broken almost every time Ally McCoist plays a Premier League match.

In December 1989 Ally scored against Motherwell to notch his 128th Premier goal and beat the previous record held by Frank McGarvey of St. Mirren and Celtic. Ally's tally just goes on growing so there is no knowing yet what the record will be when he finishes.

At the other end of the scale are players like Billy Wardle, a forward who signed professional forms for Southport in October 1936 and went on to play for Manchester City, Grimsby, Blackpool, Birmingham and Barnsley.

It took Billy ten years to score his first goal and that came from the penalty-spot in October 1946 when he was with The Mariners.

To be fair, the Second World War had something to do with Billy's goal drought, but at the end of his career in 1954, Billy had found the net just 18 times in 239 senior matches.

Dixie Dean is one of the first names people think of when they are talking about goals. Few will automatically think of Arthur Rowley, yet Arthur's goal against Bradford City when he was playing for Shrewsbury in April 1961 passed Dixie's then record of 379 League goals in a career.

Arthur didn't stop there, either. He went on to reach a grand total of 434 League goals which is a record to this day.

Of course some people are not so fortunate. Norman Wood, a forward for Stockport was playing against Fulham in a Division Two match in October 1913. In the tenth minute he scored an own goal.

Five minutes later he gave away a penalty from which Fulham made it 2-0. A few minutes later Stockport were awarded a penalty. Norman strode up to take it and missed! Fulham won 3-1.

Wilf Minter has a different tale to tell. Playing for St. Albans City against Dulwich Hamlet in a Cup replay in 1922 he scored all his side's seven goals. The only problem was, Dulwich scored eight!

Soccer fans got their money's worth on February 1st, 1936. That's the day it rained goals. There were 44 games played in the League that day and between them the 88 teams amassed 209 goals, the most ever scored in a League programme on one day.

There are often goals scored within the first minute, but Brigg's Martin Boyers has a special place in the record books for the goal he netted within four seconds.

He received the ball from the kick-off, saw that the Sheffield goalkeeper was off his line and hit the ball straight into the net.

One of our top quick-on-the-draw men must be Bryan Robson, The Manchester United star holds the record for both the fastest and second fastest Wembley goals. He scored for England against Northern Ireland after just 44 seconds when the two teams met at Wembley in 1982 and then beat his own record in December 1989, finding the net after only 38 seconds against Yugoslavia.

Teenager Mark Askwith made a name for himself in December 1992 when he scored ten goals for his Wickersley team when they beat Donfield 17-2 in the Rotherham Cup. Because the match was recognised by the Football Association, it was one for the record books.

Lots of goals often seem a thing of the past, but it was not that long ago that Manchester City beat Huddersfield 10-1 in a Division Two match. It was on November 7th 1987 and among the scorers were Tony Adcock, Paul Stewart and David White, each of whom scored a hat-trick.

So the message for this season is simple - let's have goals, goals, goals.

Three cheers for hat-trick heroes David White, Tony Adcock and Paul Stewart

Arthur Rowley still holds the League scoring record

Perfect Paul:
Villa's McGrath
is the current PFA
Player of the Year

Sweet Sheri:
Teddy was top
scorer in the
Premier with 22
last season

ACTION 94

Red Tops: Half of Manchester was singing the blues last term

Chasing shadows: Celtic and Hearts were left in the dark by Rangers

ROSS KING —

the voice of Sport on Radio 5 becomes the face in place on BBC television almost every morning as he hosts the new national television's daytime programmes during the week and fronts "The Wetter The Better" kids challenge show every Sunday morning.

But the guy who wanted to be a pro footballer just can't leave soccer alone as he tells Shoot.

ROSS ON

SHOOT: Will you be leaving your Radio 5 programmes now that you are so busy on television?
Ross King: No, I know I might be a glutton for punishment, but I couldn't just leave Fantasy Football or Go. I'm a football nut and I can't leave it alone.

Who is or was your favourite team?
Well, I come from Glasgow so you would think it would be Rangers or Celtic but in fact I have always followed Partick Thistle. The Jags are the greatest.

What is your favourite football memory?
There are several, but as a spectator I would have to say that I'll never forget the Scottish League Cup Final of 1971 when Partick were playing Celtic. I was just a little lad, but I went along with my dad, David, and my uncle Joe. I was wearing an enormous Partick scarf which some witty Celtic fans said I should have made into a suit. It was a very good-natured game and Partick won 4-1. That was fantastic. The Celtic fans couldn't believe it when we were 4-0 up at half-time. It was brilliant.

Do you have any special playing memory?
Oh yes, I hope there are more to come, but one stands out now. Everyone dreams of playing at Wembley even if they are Scottish and I played in a celebrity game for a full 90 minutes before a boys club international at the great stadium. It was England v Scotland and I scored Scotland's goal in a 1-1 draw. I must have looked really stupid because I was grinning the whole time. I couldn't get over the fact that I was playing at Wembley.

Did you play for your school?
Yes, I was captain of every school team I played for and it seemed to be a pretty safe bet that I was going to be a professional

Ross is a big Partick (stripes) fan.

footballer although I did intend also to be a PE teacher as a career back-up.

What happened — did you fail at trials?
No, it wasn't that. It's not for me to say if I would have made the grade although

some people have kindly told me I would. I just changed my mind. I had always been really keen on showbusiness and one day it just took over. Everyone freaked because they all assumed I would be a soccer pro then I just suddenly announced that I had changed my mind.

What has been your biggest soccer disappointment?
Going to Italy to watch the World Cup in 1990 and seeing Scotland dumped out. I love Italy as a country but hated it for a few minutes.

How did you set about your career?
I had a maths teacher, Roddy Hood, who helped me get into hospital broadcasting and it just took off from there. I went to bigger radio stations and then television. I've done "Run The Gauntlet", "8.15 from Manchester", "The Holiday Programme" and various others and now this.

Do you regret not going into soccer as a career?
Not really. I hope that broadcasting will give me a much longer career. Wanting a career in football is because you enjoy playing. Well, I play in lots of charity games so I have both my career and the fun of soccer.

Scotland were beaten by Costa Rica in the 1990 World Cup Finals.

THE SPOT

Do you have a favourite player?
Yes, several. Denis Law has always been a big hero. Sandy Jardine, Danny McGrain, Jim Holton — they are all great players. Today's superhero has to be Ally McCoist.

Do you have many friends in the game?
Yes, I think I make friends quite easily. One of my best pals is Ally McCoist.

What do you do in your spare time?
What spare time? I like to play football. I watch some television — Cheers, Lovejoy, crime stories — then I like to play football. I like music — especially Wet Wet Wet and I like to play football. I also enjoy going for a pasta meal and I like to play football. I like a round of golf and I like to play football. I like reading and a game of football. I like holidays in Italy and America and to play football. I also like to play tennis — oh yes, I also like to play football.

You quite like playing football then?
Only a lot!

Ally McCoist

Scotland's Denis Law is one of Ross King's heroes.

When do your new shows start?
The Wetter The Better goes out every Sunday morning at 9.40 am from October 4th. It has already been recorded at Blackpool Sand Castle and it is a lot of fun. If you don't believe me, just watch it. The daily Ross King Show starts on October 12th and is live from 9am to 1 pm.

What ambitions do you have left?
To have my photo in Shoot which I have read ever since it started. To see Scotland as World and European Champions and to see Partick take the triple and go on to win the European Cup. I'd like to score a winner at Wembley and see Ally McCoist as Prime Minister.

Any special message for readers of Shoot?
Yes, keep buying it — it's the best.

Ready

Sheri's aiming for the top again

TOTTENHAM hot-shot Teddy Sheringham wants to keep North London golden and get the boot for the second year running!

The former Millwall and Forest striker is determined to become the first-ever player to retain the SHOOT/adidas Golden Shoe for the top division's leading League scorer.

He struck gold last season with a late run which helped him see off the challenge of Les Ferdinand, Dean Holdsworth and Micky Quinn for the title of Prince of the Premier League.

Yet amazingly, his first five months at White Hart Lane produced just *five* League goals for Spurs — and two of them were penalties! But those fans who were starting to question the wisdom of his £2.1 million transfer fee were made to eat their words as the blond bombshell embarked on a sensational run of nine goals in five games. And he hasn't looked back.

"We changed our tactics just after Christmas and that really helped to bring the best out of Teddy," reveals Spurs coach Doug Livermore.

"The fact that Darren Anderton also started to find his true form helped because he supplied a great service from the wing and Teddy did the rest for us.

"Nothing he has achieved since then has surprised us because we always knew he was a quality player and now there is no better goalscorer in the country.

"His call-up to the England squad for the World Cup qualifier against Holland was well deserved and now he is looking to gain a regular international place and go to the World Cup finals with England."

Teddy's 22 goals last season means the SHOOT/adidas Golden Shoe has now been won by a Spurs or Arsenal player for six of the last seven seasons.

But though Teddy also won a Silver Boot for his 33 Second Division goals with Millwall in 1990-91, he is acutely aware that no player has ever won the honour twice in a row.

"The Golden Shoe is every striker's dream," says Teddy. "It is conclusive proof that you are the Number One. Nothing would give me greater pleasure than to receive the trophy again at the end of this season."

THE SHOOT/adidas GOLDEN SHOE WINNERS

Season	Player	Club	Goals
1981-82	Kevin Keegan	Southampton	26
1982-83	Luther Blissett	Watford	27
1983-84	Ian Rush	Liverpool	32
1984-85	Kerry Dixon	Chelsea	24
1985-86	Gary Lineker	Everton	30
1986-87	Clive Allen	Spurs	33
1987-88	John Aldridge	Liverpool	26
1988-89	Alan Smith	Arsenal	23
1989-90	Gary Lineker	Spurs	24
1990-91	Alan Smith	Arsenal	22
1991-92	Ian Wright	Arsenal	29
1992-93	Teddy Sheringham	Spurs	22

Teddy Gold!

"QUIRKY

THE things they say. It is not only the soccer commentators that say daft things. The stars themselves often say things they would rather not have let slip. Sometimes they say things which are funny at the time and sometimes things which later become quite significant. We've picked just a few quick and quirky quotes from recent season's....

"Tony Cottee will rue that wonderfully missed opportunity."
DAVID PLEAT commenting on BBC Radio 5 when Chelsea played Everton.

"Let's kill off once and for all the rumours that Ossie's job is on the line. If he leaves this club it will be of his own volition."
NEWCASTLE chairman Sir John Hall, 48 hours before Ossie Ardiles was sacked.

"We're so high in the table, our noses are bleeding."
QUEENS PARK RANGERS boss Gerry Francis when his team were riding high in the Premier League.

"I want Sheffield United to be the dirtiest, ugliest, luckiest and most boring team in the League so long as we're winning 1-0 every week."

DAVE BASSETT abandoning attempts to get his side to play pure football.

"Trevor Steven might have scored there if he'd chanced his arm with his left foot."
TREVOR BROOKING commenting for TV on England versus Denmark.

"To call Keegan a superstar is stretching a point. Skill-wise as a player there were a lot better around. He wasn't fit to lace my boots."
GEORGE BEST subtly telling us his views on Kevin Keegan.

"When you shout at your players from the bench you know you are wasting your time because you know they are not listening. You know that because you never listened when you were playing."
TERRY BUTCHER Sunderland player-manager on the problems and frustrations of being newly converted from player to manager.

'It's Wallace - no its Dorigo'
ITV's Brian Moore having trouble identifying Leeds players

QUOTES'

"On the night, it just wasn't our day."
RON ATKINSON after Villa lost to Norwich.

"The Villa chairman, Doug Ellis, told me he was right behind me. I told him I'd sooner have him in front of me where I can see him."
TOMMY DOCHERTY on his time as Villa manager.

"Football hooligans? Well there are 92 club chairmen for a start."
BRIAN CLOUGH discussing football's problems.

POTTY

MANCHESTER UNITED, Liverpool, Arsenal, Tottenham and the rest beware - Stoke City are aiming to shoot you down in flames.

The Potters' wheel has turned almost full circle since 1985, when Stoke crashed out of the then Division One and dropped like a

stone to Division Three.

But now they are back with the big boys, and last year's Second Division Champions, who boast bigger attendances than many Premier League clubs, reckon they can go all the way to the top.

"We're on our way back," blasts goalkeeper Peter Fox, the only survivor from Stoke's last spell in the top flight.

"There's a belief about the club, and who knows what we can achieve now. Stoke can become a force to be reckoned with in the next few seasons."

After several years in the doldrums, City announced their intentions by appointing former Manchester United and Scotland star Lou Macari as manager in June 1991.

Macari, who cut his managerial teeth with Swindon, West Ham and Birmingham, led the club to victory in the 1992 Autoglass Trophy - their first success since the 1972 League Cup - and hasn't looked back since.

The Scot instilled good habits into his young players, and a blend of simple passing, high speed movement and one hundred per cent effort blasted Stoke into orbit and landed them the 1992/93 Second Division title.

Players such as last season's top scorer Mark Stein, and tricky winger Kevin Russell have clearly benefitted from Macari's insistence on playing the game 'the right way'.

But the manager refuses to take all the credit for The Potters' turnaround in fortunes.

"The reason we've been so successful on the field is because we have the right set-up off it," insists Macari.

"A lot of our success has stemmed from the players self-belief. We had an awful start to last season, but suddenly everything clicked and we just kept on winning.

"We're not kidding ourselves about the future - we've got a lot of hard work ahead. But it's a relief to be back on the right track.

"At a big club like Stoke it's impossible for one person to do everything. I'm very lucky to have

TIME

people like Chic Bates and Pete Henderson around to help out.

Another reason behind Stoke's tremendous form has been their ability to score goals from anywhere.

Despite Mark Stein's return of 26 League goals last season, no player is asked to take sole responsibility for goalscoring.

"We don't have to rely solely on our strikers coming up with the goods," admits assistance manager Bates.

"All our players are happy on the ball and comfortable going for goal.

"We pride ourselves on the players' fitness, but we also realise that putting the ball in the net is the most important thing, and we do a lot of work with the ball in training.

"We have a method we believe works, and we are not going to change it.

"Why change a winning formula?"

Vale of Cheers!

ANOTHER man delighted to see the recent revival at the Victoria Ground is John Rudge, manager of local rivals Port Vale.

Vale chased Stoke all the way for last season's Second Division title, but ended up having to endure the Play-Offs as they slipped out of the automatic promotion places in the last week of the season.

But Rudge insists that Stoke's performances can only be good for Potteries football.

"We played Stoke five times last year - and all the matches were great for everyone.

"We both got our highest crowds of the season in the local derbies, and it was great to see real local interest.

"The atmosphere of those games has rubbed off on the players and they want to experience big matches every week."

Club File

Formed: 1863 (founder members of Football League 1888).

Colours: Red/White striped shirts, white shorts, white socks.

Biggest fee received: £750,000 from Everton for Peter Beagrie.

Biggest fee paid: £480,000 to Sheff Wed for Ian Cranson.

Honours: Champions Div 2 1932/33, 1962/63 and 1992/93; Champions Div 3N 1926/27; League Cup winners 1972; Watney Cup winners 1973; Autoglass Trophy winners 1992.

ODD SPOT

KEEN punters could do worse than put a few quid on Stoke to lift the Second Division Championship trophy in 2023.

The club have made a habit of winning the Second Division every thirty years - 1932-33, 1962/63 and 1992/93. So if The Potters stick to form, then the 2022/23 season should end in glory!

TAKE YOUR PICK

1. Which club won the 1989 FA Cup Final?
a) Everton b) Liverpool c) Arsenal

2. Who scored the winning goal in the 1986 World Cup Final (right)?
a) Burruchaga b) Maradona
c) Valdano

3. Which former England star is nicknamed Razor?
a) Ray Wilkins b) Gary Lineker
c) Kevin Keegan

4. Who was the manager at Aston Villa before Ron Atkinson?
a) Graham Taylor b) Jo Venglos
c) Peter Withe

5. Roland Nilsson (below) is capped by which country?
a) Norway b) Sweden c) Denmark

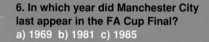

6. In which year did Manchester City last appear in the FA Cup Final?
a) 1969 b) 1981 c) 1985

7. Where do Hull play their home games?
a) Bootham Crescent b) Boothferry Park c) Boundary Park

8. Which club was relegated from the Premier League alongside Palace and Forest last season?
a) Middlesbrough b) Leicester
c) Luton

9. For which Italian club did Andy Moller play last season?
a) Juventus b) Inter Milan c) Torino

10. Who won the Milk Cup in 1986?
a) QPR b) Oxford c) Norwich

11. Which club did George Graham (left) leave to manage Arsenal?
a) Millwall b) Brentford c) L.Orient

12. Who broke Newcastle's run of 11 straight wins in the First Division last season?
a) Leicester   b) Grimsby c) West Ham

Three alternative answers are given to each question. Can you pick the right one.

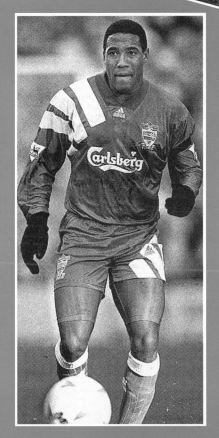

13. Gianluigi Lentini became the most expensive player in the world when he left which club to join Milan?
a) Fiorentina b) Torino c) Lazio

14. Who did Rangers beat in the 1992 Skol Cup Final?
a) Celtic b) Hearts c) Aberdeen

15. With which player did Carl Griffiths share the SHOOT/adidas Golden Shoe for the leading scorer in the Third Division last term?
a) Wayne Clarke b) Tony Naylor
c) Darren Foreman

16. What did Brian Deane do last year that put him in the record books?
a) Scored the first goal in the Premier League b) Scored the fastest goal in history c) First player to be sent-off twice in the same game

17. Who lost their first League game at their home ground in seven years in 1992?
a) Leeds b) AC Milan c) Charlton

18. They play at the Goldstone Ground and Cloughie managed them. Who are they?
a) Brighton b) Hartlepool c) Wolves

19. How many goals did Gary Lineker (below) score in Italia 90?
a) Four b) Five c) Six

20. Who did Manchester United (above) beat to win the 1991 European Cup-Winners' Cup Final?
a) Real Madrid b) Juventus
c) Barcelona

21. Ally McCoist played for one English League club. Name them.
a) Sunderland b) Newcastle
c) Middlesbrough

22. What is John Barnes' nickname?
a) Flintstone b) Trigger c) Digger

23. Enzo Scifo is an international for which country?
a) France b) Belgium c) Italy

24. Who finished runners-up in the Scottish Premier League in 1992-93?
a) Aberdeen b) Hearts c) Dundee Utd

25. Which club did Chris Waddle leave to join Sheffield Wednesday?
a) Marseille b) Monaco c) Nantes

Answers on page 125

GLYN HODGES
SHEFFIELD UTD

GIANT CROSSWORD

DOWN

ACROSS

Stars reveal their...
CLAIM TO FAME

HAVE you ever been mistaken for someone else? Is your cousin famous? Those are just two of the Claims To Fame by some of today's top soccer stars who are not only well-known because of playing football, but have another string to their bow — something else that makes them the centre of attraction at parties.

PAUL INCE *(Manchester United):*
"My claim to fame is that Nigel Benn, the World Champion boxer is my cousin. I fancied having a go at boxing myself and used to do a bit before I got seriously into soccer. I like to go to boxing matches and was once mistaken for Sugar Ray Leonard, which was very flattering. He is one of the greatest boxers of all time."

TONY DALEY *(Aston Villa):*
"My claim to fame is that I once met Uri Geller and watched him do one of his spoon bending stunts in front of my very eyes. It was really amazing and hard to believe what I was seeing. I have met several famous people, but that was really something."

ALLY McCOIST *(Rangers):*
"A lot of people say I am famous for jokes, but my real claim to fame is that I have a lot of friends in showbusiness, especially in Scotland. Among my best pals are Wet Wet Wet and I have appeared on stage with them. If I hadn't been a footballer, I wouldn't have minded being in the pop business. I have made records, but not as a serious attempt at becoming a pop star."

LEE DIXON (Arsenal):
"My claim to fame is to do with golf. I haven't been mistaken for anyone else, but I did once play golf with Bruce Forsyth. As well as being a great entertainer, he is a brilliant golfer and I'm sure he could have been a professional. It was an experience playing against him and a real claim to fame."

GARY SPEED (Leeds United):
"I love being a professional footballer, but if I could have another claim to fame, I would like to have made it as a cricketer. I played for Wales as a schoolboy and everyone said that I could go all the way to Test cricket. I chose football and don't regret that. It's a pity that you can't do both sports because I could have played for Wales as a soccer international and possibly have played for England at cricket."

JOHN HARKES (Sheff Wednesday):
"A lot of people keep on about me being the first American to play in the FA Cup Final, but my real claim to fame is that I used to be a ball boy at New York Cosmos when Pele and Beckenbauer were there. We used to share a dressing room so my claim to fame is that I got changed with Pele."

GARY MABBUTT (Tottenham):
"Apart from being a footballer I am probably best known as being a diabetic. I get loads of letters from people asking for advice. I have to have my own secretary to answer them all. I suppose that is a sort of claim to fame, but I have another — I once met Chris De Burgh's mum and dad while on holiday in Florida."

CHRIS WADDLE (Sheff. Wednesday):
"My claim to fame, apart from once working in a sausage factory, is that I appeared on Top Of The Pops with Glenn Hoddle. We had a record in the charts and had to go on TOTP to promote it. It was a bit nerve-wracking and it was a bit embarrassing becuase you had to mime everything. But it was something I shall never forget and was my moment of fame."

TEDDY SHERINGHAM (Tottenham):
"My claim to fame is a case of mistaken identity. I like to play golf and someone once came up to me and asked for an autograph while I was at a golf club.

The problem was that he thought I was Nick Faldo. It wasn't because I am any good at golf, he thought we looked the same. I wouldn't his golf skills!"

GARY STEVENS (Rangers):
"I don't know if it is a real claim to fame, but a lot of other people seem to think so. I play the saxaphone and like jazz. I sometimes join other musicians to play in clubs. I'll let the others judge whether or not I'm any good, but it seems to go down well with most people. My Rangers team-mates often make requests — but I'm going to carry on playing anyway."

ROBERT FLECK (Chelsea):
"My claim to fame is that I played snooker against Steve Davis. He is a great guy and a brilliant player. I didn't beat him, of course, but at least I can say that I played against him."

MATT LE TISSIER

SOUTHAMPTON

TOO BIG FOR HIS BOOTS!

ALL wingers like a big target man - and they don't come much larger than 25-year-old Kevin Francis at Stockport County who stands head and shoulders above his opponents.

Kevin is in the League record books as the No. 1 giant in English football. He stands at 6ft 7in, wears size 13 boots - and scores plenty of goals.

"I've always been tall. I was big as a baby and was always the biggest in my age group at school," he says.

"But when I was playing at school they were very strict on ages and I always played in my age group - there was never any attempt to play me against older boys.

"It was a bit different in Saturday and Sunday League football."

Kevin, born in Moseley, in Birmingham, started out at non-league Mile Oak Rovers before joining Derby where he made only a handful of appearances in three seasons .

He then moved to Stockport and has not looked back.

"There are some disadvantages in being so tall. One is that I get picked out on the football pitch and not always for the right reasons," he said.

"There are always people who want to have a pop at me and it is something I have learned to handle.

Priceless

"Then there are occasions when I take my height for granted and wait for the cross to reach me without jumping. Nothing makes me more angry with myself then when I stand rooted to the spot and let a defender come in and out-leap me."

Kevin, however, is forgiven the odd lapse by his manager Danny Bergara who describes him as a "priceless" asset to the club.

"He's been very good for us and has scored a lot of goals," said Bergara. "Sometimes we expect too much from him and we have to remember he's not a machine."

Kevin may be able to look after himself on the pitch but it is a different story at home with his 5ft 2in wife Sharon, and baby daughter.

"They both bully me around and I do as I am told," said Kevin. "But that's women for you!"

NIALL QUINN

MAN CITY

SO YOU call yourself a soccer fan, eh? Well, let's see what you are really made of. Put your hat and scarf on and try this simple test to find out if you are a real fan, a super fan, a mega fan or a supermegafantasmagical sensational fan. Just pick the most suitable answers to these scientifically selected posers, specially chosen by our fan computer.

RU A

1. Your house is on fire. What do you grab before you get out? Would it be:
(A) Your signed photo of Bryan Robson?
(B) Your ticket for a Kylie Minogue concert?
(C) Your insurance policy?

2. There's a general election. Do you vote for:
(A) The politician who supports your team?
(B) The politician who wears the right colour rosette?
(C) The politician who admits to knowing nothing about football?

3. Your favourite player gets injured through his own clumsiness. Do you:
(A) Send him a get well card?
(B) Write and tell him he's an idiot?
(C) Buy him a year's subscription to BUPA?

4. You hear that your club might go bust. Do you:
(A) Start a fund-raising campaign?
(B) Support someone else?
(C) Write to the newspapers and complain?

5. You ask a star player for his autograph and he ignores you. Do you:
(A) Run after him and ask again?
(B) Tell him you had mistaken him for someone else anyway?
(C) Forget it and resolve to ask him another day?

6. A friend gives you a Cup Final ticket, even though your team is not in the Final. Do you:
(A) Keep it and go to the match?
(B) Sell it for more than face value?
(C) Pass it on to someone who does support one of the teams involved?

7. You are sitting next to a rival fan and your team is losing 6-0 at half time. Do you:
A) Congratulate him on his team's play?
(B) Ask him if he is sitting in the right seat?
(C) Leave?

So that's how he got elected!

FANATIC?

England win the World Cup...you'll be lucky

'The referee's a nice guy...'

8. The referee refuses your side a definite penalty? Do you:

(A) Say, never mind?

(B) Recommend an optician?

(C) Question his knowledge of the game?

9. The opposition striker misses a sitter. Do you:

(A) Laugh?

(B) Wish him better luck next time?

(C) Moan at your own defence?

10. England win the World Cup. Do you:

(A) Tell everyone you always knew they would?

(B) Admit you were wrong?

(C) Ask the nearest person if you are alive or have arrived in heaven?

11. You are offered a choice of presents. Do you:

(A) Go for the gold Mercedes?

(B) Accept a holiday in Barbados?

(C) Take a year's subscription to Shoot?

12. Your manager is sacked. Do you:

(A) Send him a sympathy note?

(B) Send the chairman a poison pen letter?

(C) Apply for his job?

continued overleaf ➡

RU A FANATIC?

13. Your girlfriend supports your rivals. Do you:

(A) Try to educate and convert her?

(B) Marry her and insist she follows your team?

(C) Get another girlfriend?

14. A scout from Rochdale comes to see you play. Do you:

(A) Play your best?

(B) Pretend you are injured?

(C) Give him a false name?

15. You see Gazza in a restaurant. Do you:

(A) Ask for an autograph?

(B) Discuss the finer points of Italian opera?

(C) Tell him you're Jeremy Beadle in disguise?

Now have a look at the answers and count your points tally.

ANSWERS

1. (A). 10 - that has to be a prized possession.
    (B). 0 - easily replaced.
    (C). 5 - boring but sensible.

2. A). 5 - at least you've got something in common.
    (B). 0 - he takes the rosette off when he gets home.
    (C). 10 - you know what to expect.

3. (A). 10 - nice to know someone cares.
    (B). 0 - he already knows that.
    (C). 5 - he's probably already got one, but the thought's there.

4. (A). 10 - that's what being a supporter is all about.
    (B). 5 - depends who it is!
    (C). 0 - be more helpful to send the stamps to the club.

5. (A). 5 - he might not have heard you.
    (B). 0 - he might have something else on his mind.
    (C). 10 - good thinking. He'll probably sign next time.

6. (A). 10 - don't blame you.
    (B). 10 - how could you!
    (C). 20 - now that's a real fan!

7. (A). 0 - hypocrite!
    (B). 5 - one way to break the ice.
    (C). 10 - now that's a real fan.

8. (A). 10 - even if you don't mean it.
    (B). 5 - you never know he might be grateful.
    (C). 0 - what's his soccer know-how got to do with being blind?

9. (A). 10 - honesty is always the best policy.
    (B). 5 - he might be signed by your team.
    (C). 0 - did you expect them to score for him as well?!

10. (A). 0 - don't tell lies.
    (B). 10 - well, you were, weren't you?
    (C). 0?- ye of little faith.

11. (A). 0 - motor insurance too expensive.
    (B). 5 - there might be a match on.
    (C). 10 - what did you expect?

12. (A). 5 - he did try.
    (B). 0 - he might not eat it.
    (C). 10 - that's what football is all about.

13. (A). 10 - no harm in trying.
    (B). 0 - better to walk into a Celtic pub wearing a Rangers scarf.
    (C). 5 - some thing's just don't work out.

14. (A). 5 - be a good sport.
    (B). 0 - you do that AFTER you've turned professional.
    (C). 10 - they might think they've really got the new George Best.

15. (A). 10 - a real fan couldn't resist it.
    (B). 5 - why not, he might NOT think that Nessun Dorma is a Japanese car.
    (C). 0 - nobody would admit that.

So how did you get on? Add up your points and see which category is yours.

0- 50 -You must be a real fan to have this book.

51- 75 -OK clever clogs, we'll admit you're a superfan.

75-100 -Sell your story to the newspapers, you're a megafan.

100-150 -Try not to pull a muscle as you pat yourself on the back, you're a super megafantasmagicalsensationalfan!!!!!

JULIAN JOACHIM

LEICESTER

DAVID O'LEARY'S 20

DAVID O'LEARY has proved throughout his magnificent career that nice guys do not always finish second.

The genial Irishman, one of the most loved and respected players in modern football, ended his glittering Arsenal career in the style befitting the club's greatest servant — carrying the FA Cup around Wembley.

O'Leary, Arsenal's longest serving player, completed 20 years service at Highbury on May 5, 1993. Two weeks later he had a fairytale ending to his final game in the red and white of Arsenal as they beat Sheffield Wednesday in the FA Cup Final replay.

And nobody can have failed to be

'Man United wanted me!'

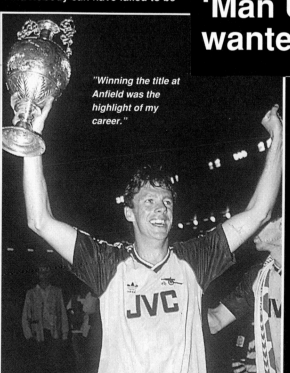

"Winning the title at Anfield was the highlight of my career."

What a time to score your first goal for your country - in a World Cup penalty shoot-out!

Glorious Years

moved as O'Leary walked down the steps from Wembley's Royal Box cradling the FA Cup in his arms. He'd finished his last season for The Gunners with winners' medals from both domestic Cup Finals, another first in a long list of achievements that few players can match.

O'Leary first walked into Highbury as a star-struck 14-year-old schoolboy in 1973.

"I fell in love with the place as soon as I saw it," he says. "Manchester United also wanted me but I had no hesitation joining Arsenal, who had two other Dublin boys - Liam Brady and Frank Stapleton."

Although he was born just down the road from Highbury, in Stoke Newington, his family returned to Dublin before young David's first birthday. Under previous nationality rules, that would have meant him playing for England rather than the Republic of Ireland.

But it was the luck of the Irish to get O'Leary, who is now one of their most-capped players with well over 60 international

appearances. And it was easy to pick out the highlight of his career with the Republic of Ireland.

"It has to be the 1990 World Cup," he admits. "I scored the decisive penalty in the shoot-out against Romania, taking us through to meet Italy in the Quarter-Finals.

"I would love to go to the US for the 1994 Finals."

His club highlights were harder to choose, with two League titles, two FA Cups and two League Cups, but he plumps for the win at Anfield that clinched the 1989 title.

"To beat Liverpool in the dying seconds and take the Championship from them was fantastic," he says. "I'd been at Arsenal for 16 years and was sick of hearing how the double-winning side had clinched the title by beating Spurs at White Hart Lane in 1971."

It was a well-deserved reward for O'Leary, whose service to Arsenal was praised by manager George Graham: "His loyalty is a rare commodity in football these days."

A measure of the high regard commanded by O'Leary was that Arsenal gave him a second testimonial, in between the FA Cup Final and replay. There were tears from O'Leary and many of the 23,000 fans, about whom he said: "You can't buy that sort of relationship."

The Premier League's inaugural Champions Manchester United were the opponents and their skipper Bryan Robson said: "In these days of big incentives it is easy to be persuaded to move on because of the money. But David has stayed loyal."

O'Leary says simply: "I never wanted to play for anyone else, although I had plenty of offers when my contracts were up."

Now he is embarking on the second phase of his career after a record 722 appearances for Arsenal. The club and the shirt may have changed, but David O'Leary will still be football's Mr Nice Guy.

There were a few tears at David's testimonial v Man United

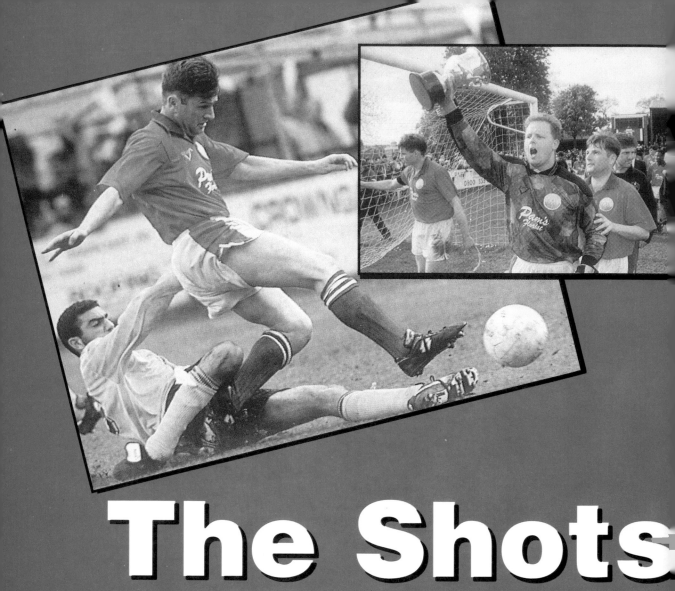

The Shots

WHAT happened next for the two football clubs who became victims of the 1990s recession?

For one of them, Aldershot, there is life after League football and they hope to rise like the phoenix - the emblem of their club shirts - to new heights.

A bird also has its place in the history of the other team - Maidstone - they are as dead as the dodo.

Aldershot became the first League team to bite the dust since 1962 and the death of Accrington Stanley in March 1992.

Less than six months later, Maidstone were joining them on the rocky road to ruin. Rumoured to have debits in the region of £650,000 they could not give the required assurance that they would fulfil their fixtures and were forced to resign. The team broke-up and the club is defunct. It was the end of a 95-year quest for bigger and greater things.

Aldershot, on the other hand, regrouped and helped by the financial acumen of new chairman Terry Owens and the management of Steve Wignall, a former player, won a place in the Diadora Third Division - five leagues down from the pro ranks.

So far, so good for Aldershot who were crowned Champions after their first season in new surroundings.

"I have a 10-year-plan for the club with the aim of regaining League status and while I don't expect us to win titles every season I do expect us to be promoted," said Owens.

"I have been a supporter for 40 years. What is essential is that everything we do is on a firm financial footing."

All the professional players have gone and overheads have been drastically reduced by the more parochial travelling demands of the Diadora League.

Wignall has been signed on a two-year contract and the club scours the

Steve Wignall

Rise Again!

immediate area for new players. Aldershot are made up of locals and the farthest anyone travels to play for them is from Basingstoke.

"We like to pass the ball but some of the grounds we now visit are not good enough for that sort of play because the clubs do not have the finances to maintain the pitches .

Cinderella

"I'm told the Diadora Second Division is even more physical but there is a great team spirit here and there is no reason why we cannot climb up and up again."

Wimbledon made a name as the Cinderella club of football, rising in 1977 as newly-elected members of the Fourth Division to almost permanent status in the top flight.

That is the shining example, however hard times become, that all clubs outside football cling to. The dream can become reality.

PAT NEVIN
TRANMERE

RANGERS RULE

Scottish Cup winners - 1993

Arsenal - FA Cup and Coca-Cola Cup winners 1993

DOUBLE CUP KINGS

SCOTLAND might freeze each winter but Hogmanay is definitely HOT if you are a Rangers or a Celtic fan because the traditional New Year Old Firm clash is the fiercest fixture in football.

Forget about the other derbies, they don't come any more passionate than the rivalry between the two sides of Glasgow.

This season the annual shoot-out will be hosted by Celtic and The Bhoys will be stirring the cauldron to make sure that the men from Ibrox have the warmest of welcomes and the unhappiest of New Years.

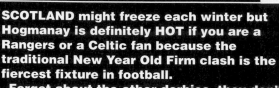

WE have to turn the clock back to the last century to see how it all began.

Rangers were the first club to be formed. They sprang to life in 1873 when a group of rowers used to kick a ball about for fun after their stints on the River Clyde.

Rangers' first ground was at Glasgow Green which is still a centre for rowing enthusiasts.

Celtic were formed in 1887 by Brother Walfrid of the Catholic teaching order of Marist Brothers.

Celtic Football and Athletic Club was initially formed to raise money for food for needy Irish Catholic children in the poor east end of the city.

While Celtic were die-hard Catholic, Rangers were less religiously starched, but the religious rivalry grew up with the clubs.

The first match was in November 1888. Celtic won 5-2. Since then the matches between the two sides have thrown up some amazing stories and results — and the rivalry goes on!

- **During** the 1889-90 season Rangers won every Scottish League and Cup game they played — except the Cup Final which they lost 2-0 to Celtic.
- **Rangers** have four times done the treble of League, League Cup and Scottish Cup — Celtic have done it twice.
- **Rangers** are the most successful team in the world in terms of the number of domestic trophies won.
- **Celtic** hold the record for being the most successful club in Britain in any one season. During the 1966-67 campaign they won the Championship, League Cup, Scottish Cup, Glasgow Cup and the European Cup.
- **Celtic** still hold the record of 62 League matches without defeat from November 13th 1915 to April 21st 1917.

- **The** biggest crowd at a Scottish League Cup-tie was the 127,609 who crammed into Hampden Park for the Final on October 23rd, 1965 to see Celtic beat Rangers 2-1.
- **Celtic's** record attendance was set at 92,000 when Rangers were the visitors for a League match on January 31st, 1938. Celtic won 3-0.
- **Rangers** record attendance is 118,567 set on January 2nd, 1939. The visitors were, of course, Celtic and the score was 2-1 to Rangers.
- **On** March 22nd, 1986 the two clubs shared their highest-scoring draw - 4-4 at Ibrox.
- **Rangers** biggest win over Celtic at Ibrox was the 5-0 success in the 1893-94 season. Four seasons later Celtic had their best win at Ibrox with a 4-0 revenge.

MANAY

• **At** Parkhead Celtic have twice beaten Rangers 6-2 while Rangers once won there 5-1, the highest scores by the clubs at Celtic.

•**The** biggest-ever winning score in the Scottish League Cup Final was on October 19th, 1957 when Celtic and Rangers met in the Final for the first time. Celtic won by a record 7-1 and reports say that if the Rangers keeper had not been in such good form it could have been double figures.

• **When** Rangers won the League Championship with a record 76 points in the 1920-21 season their only defeat was on New Year's day when Celtic beat them 2-0 at Ibrox.

• **In** 1973 Alfie Conn won a Scottish Cup winners medal playing for Rangers who beat Celtic 3-2 in the Final. In the 1977 Final he was a winner again — this time playing for Celtic in a 1-0 win over Rangers!

• **The** atmosphere at an Old Firm Clash is white hot, but it really boiled over in 1909 when the Scottish Cup was withheld because of a riot. Rangers and

September 5th, 1931 was marred when Celtic's 'keeper John Thomson was knocked unconscious in a collision and taken to hospital where he died later that evening.

• **The** rivalry has become more intense for this season's Hogmanay clash because Rangers have now won the Premier League title five times in a row, the best run since Celtic's nine-title span from 1966 to 1974.

Results of Old Firm Hogmanay Clashes during the last ten years

1993	Rangers 1, Celtic 0.
1992	Celtic 1, Rangers 3.
1991	Rangers 2, Celtic 0.
1990	Celtic 0, Rangers 1.
1989	Rangers 4, Celtic 1.
1988	Celtic 2, Rangers 0.
1987	Rangers 2, Celtic 0.
1986	Celtic 2, Rangers 0.
1985	Rangers 1, Celtic 2.
1984	Celtic 3, Rangers 0.

Celtic had twice drawn 2-2 and then 1-1. At the end of the second match the fans went on the rampage because they suspected that a draw had been arranged to ensure more gate money from a third match. The Scottish FA decided to abandon the competition at that stage.

• **Tragedy** struck at Ibrox on January 2nd, 1971 when the Hogmanay match became a disaster. There were 66 people killed and many more injured when the crowd tumbled down the terracing.

• **The** Old Firm clash on

THE religious fervour between the two clubs has been broken several times.

In the 1920's Rangers had a Catholic player and there have been several since.

Celtic have been fairly happy to go outside their religious ranks to engage the best talent and were never more happy than when they had a Protestant manager — Jock Stein, who took them all the way to the European Cup.

In recent times the most famous switch came when Mo Johnson made his name with Celtic, moved abroad and then came back, apparently to rejoin Celtic, but finally signing for Rangers.

"Everything happened very quickly and when the opportunity came to join Graeme Souness I saw it as a brilliant chance and a really good career move," said Mo.

He, of course, knows better than most just how hot things get in Glasgow when the Old Firm clash.

"I still cannot understand why the rivalry is so intense between the fans. The

Rangers and Celtic fans all live and work together, but once they go through the turnstiles it is completely different.

"I would love to see the Glasgow derbies played in the same spirit as the Mersey derbies.

"In Glasgow when you play for Partick Thistle then everybody is your friend. But when you join Rangers or Celtic half the city is against you."

Mo Johnston: From Green God to True Blue

BOSNICH

Glad he quit Bondi beach for Birmingham

WHEN it comes to sun, sand and surf, Birmingham isn't exactly the place to be. And perhaps that's just as well for Aston Villa goalkeeper Mark Bosnich.

For it was too much of the Bondi beach lifestyle which almost wrecked the young Aussie's career before it had even got off the ground.

Bosnich first came to prominence with his outstanding displays for Australia in the 1991 World Youth Championships in Portugal, when his agility and confidence helped the soccer novices reach the Semi-Finals.

Manchester United heard of the promising youngster and signed him up for a six-month loan period. He even made three senior appearances for Alex Ferguson before work permit problems ended his dreams of Old Trafford stardom.

And that's when his problems really started.

Back home in Sydney, the drop in playing standards and the temptation of the good life started to have a damaging effect on the disillusioned youngster.

"Australia is a very hard place to discipline yourself because there are so many great temptations," he reveals.

"It's very easy to go overboard and I had too much of a good time. I was only training three nights a week and spending all day on the beach.

"My weight shot up to more than 14 stone because I was eating and drinking too much and after things looking so good with United I could suddenly see my career just fizzling out.

"Playing for Sydney Croatia just wasn't the same as playing in the English First Division and my own standards were starting to suffer. That's when I realised I had to get back to England if I was going to make a name for myself."

Luckily for Bosnich, fiancee Lisa just happened to have been born in England. So when they got married in February, 1992, his work permit problems suddenly disappeared.

The ultra-confident Bosnich had always remained in touch with former United coach Brian Whitehouse, who had since moved to Aston Villa. So when he suddenly became eligible for a return to British football, Villa moved in.

Villa boss Ron Atkinson is delighted with his transfer coup. "Mark has been phenomenal," he says. "His attitude is first class and he shows no nerves."

Nor does Bosnich have any regrets about his decision to join Villa. "I was really devastated when I wasn't allowed to sign for United and thought my chances of becoming a player in the Premier League were over," he admits.

"I still can't believe I'm back and doing so well with another giant club."

WARHURST OUTBURST!

PAUL WARHURST is determined to shake off the image of being too versatile for his own good and make a name for himself in the England team *as a defender*.

The Sheffield Wednesday star insists that he is an out and out goal-stopper with no interest in transferring his talents up to the other end of the pitch as a goal-taker.

But Paul's problem is that he's simply too good up front for Owls boss Trevor Francis to completely rule him out of his attacking options.

Warhurst's secret nose for goal first came to light in September 1992 when an injury to David Hirst called for desperate measures.

Aided by his exceptional pace and coolness under pressure, Paul hammered five goals in eight games before reverting to his usual position in defence.

So when injuries struck again in

January, Francis didn't have to think twice about switching the 24-year-old star back into the firing line, where a further burst of 12 goals in as many games not only helped Wednesday to two Cup Finals but also earned him a call-up to Graham Taylor's England squad.

Yet, amazingly, before that first goal of the season in a 2-1 win at Nottingham Forest, Warhurst had never scored for Wednesday in 41 games for the club.

Furthermore, his three years at Oldham before a £750,000 transfer to Hillsborough had produced only two goals in 86 games. And his first club, Manchester City, didn't even give him a single game before flogging him off for a mere £10,000.

Yet the quiet man of Wednesday is adamant that his long-term future is in defence.

"I'm more than happy to help out in attack when the situation demands, but I still reckon I'm a better defender than forward," he insists.

"It was a very strange feeling to suddenly score all those goals last season. When I found myself in a scoring position I just did what came naturally and it seemed to pay off."

But if the modest Warhurst, who has overcome the handicap of asthma to carve out a successful Premier League career, plays down his attacking achievements, others are more willing to sing his praises.

"Paul tells me that he doesn't really enjoy playing up front but he looks as if he's been a forward all his life," says Francis.

And Wednesday striker Mark Bright has no doubts about Warhurst's ability to survive at the very top level as a forward.

"It was a bit of a laugh at first when Paul started scoring all those goals last season," he reveals.

"Hirsty and I would be sitting on the bench nudging each other and saying `we'll never get back in the side now'. But as the goals kept going in, it suddenly didn't seem so funny.

"Now we all know that Paul is a serious rival for a place in our forward line — even if he doesn't see it that way."

'd rather stop 'em than score 'em

Those were the days of goals, goals and more goals.

THE younger generations miss a lot of football fun around Christmas nowadays.

Back when your dad was a lad there used to be a full programme of matches on Christmas Day and on Boxing Day, unless one fell on a Sunday.

In those happy times you could catch a train or a bus on Christmas Day to a match, usually played in the morning, and still get home in time for the traditional turkey and plum pudding.

That's all changed, of course, and not surprisingly, because of transport difficulties and the understandable pleas from players, officials and club employees to have time off.

Matches over Christmas used to have an atmosphere all their own.

For example, the record number of goals ever scored in a single Football League game happened on a Boxing Day. That was in the Third Division North in 1935, when Tranmere — who had lost 4-1 at Oldham on the previous day — won the return match 13-4.

Four years earlier, Tranmere beat Rochdale 9-1 on Christmas Day and lost the return 6-3 on Boxing Day. That total of 19 goals was the highest scored between the same two clubs in the same season, and so it remained

FESTIVE

Be

The Hammers were hammered 8-2 by Blackburn on Boxing Day, 1963

FUN

until the 1959-60 season.

Then there was a remarkable reversal in the Second Division matches between Plymouth and Charlton.

Argyle won 6-4 at home, and Charlton in turn won 6-4 at home. The dates? December 25 and December 26, of course.

The record victory in a Fourth Division match was set on Boxing Day 1962, when Oldham hammered Southport 11-0. Bert Lister scored six, which also remains the individual record for Division Four.

The festive fun led to some unusual turnabouts. In 1926, for example, Luton beat Millwall 6-0 at home in the Third Division South on Christmas Day, only to lose 7-0 at The Den on the following afternoon.

In 1932 Everton beat Sunderland 6-2 at Goodison, and the teams spent Christmas night travelling to Wearside together for the return next day. Perhaps Everton celebrated too well while on the trip, for Sunderland won 7-0.

How about this for a topsy-turvy double? Second Division 1956: Bury 7 Bristol Rovers 2, then Bristol Rovers 6 Bury 1. Over Christmas, of course.

And then there's the First Division overall scoring record of 66 goals in 10 games, on Boxing Day 1963. The results included Fulham 10 Ipswich 1 and West Ham 2 Blackburn 8.

Those were the days!

Graham Leggat – Fulham hot-shot

Rangers have virtually made the Scottish Premier Division trophy their own property. They've won it for the last five years.

Shoot! Annual 1994 is published by IPC Magazines Ltd., IPC Specialist Group, 25th Floor, King's Reach Tower, Stamford Street, London SE1 9LS. Shoot! Annual must not be sold at more than the recommended selling price shown on page three. Sole agents for Australia and New Zealand: Gordon & Gotch Ltd. South Africa: Central News Agency. All rights reserved and reproduction without permission strictly forbidden. Printed in England by BPCC Paulton Books Ltd., Bletchley. Typesetting and origination by Meridian Media Services, Peterborough. Distributed by IPC Marketforce.